More Praise f

"In *Sidewalk Oracles*, Robert Moss removes the veil separating us from the underlying patterns and processes that provide meaning, direction, and joyful wonder in life. This book is urgently needed as an antidote to the deadening chorus of materialistic science that tells us there is no purpose or direction in our world, and intention and will are illusions. *Sidewalk Oracles* is CPR for the soul."

— Larry Dossey, MD, author of
*One Mind: How Our Individual Mind Is
Part of a Greater Consciousness and Why It Matters*

"*Sidewalk Oracles* grabbed me in the first five pages. The historical perspective and broad scope of meaning that Robert Moss brings to his readers are instructive — even enlightening. After using his eighteen games for playing with signs, symbols, and synchronicity, I can attest to the incredible value, as well as delight, in following his guidance. This book is inspiring and indeed brings us to 'discern interweavings of energy presences from different realities and the crisscrossing of event tracks from parallel worlds.' This book will instruct you in how to walk in this expanded reality with a new awareness, a new ability to notice assistance all around you, and a joyful skip in your step."

— Joyce Hawkes, PhD, author of *Cell-Level Healing*

Praise for Robert Moss

"Writing about dreams, Moss is eloquent and authoritative, a wise teacher." — *Publishers Weekly*

"[*The Secret History of Dreaming* is] captivating, well written, and sure to please." — *Library Journal*

"*The Boy Who Died and Came Back* is a masterpiece."
— Bonnie Horrigan, author of *Red Moon Passage*

SIDEWALK ORACLES

SIDEWALK ORACLES

PLAYING WITH SIGNS, SYMBOLS, AND SYNCHRONICITY IN EVERYDAY LIFE

ROBERT MOSS

New World Library
Novato, California

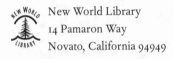 New World Library
14 Pamaron Way
Novato, California 94949

Text design by Tona Pearce Myers

Library of Congress Cataloging-in-Publication Data is available.

First printing, October 2015
ISBN 978-1-60868-336-9
Printed in Canada on 100% postconsumer-waste recycled paper

 New World Library is proud to be a Gold Certified Environmentally Responsible Publisher. Publisher certification awarded by Green Press Initiative. www.greenpressinitiative.org

10   9   8   7   6   5   4   3   2   1

CONTENTS

PROLOGUE

THE SPEAKING LAND

Everything is speaking to you.
The tarot Fool is out of the deck
and walking up the drive
with the patterns of the world in his sack
to remind you (if you'll listen)
that to be wise you may need to be crazy
in the eyes of others — and not confuse this
with behaving like a bloody fool.

The chickens in the yard can teach you
multiplication and what you need
to hatch that dragon's egg you have inside.
Hawk will come over, more interested in you
than a chicken dinner. Are you ready
to soar on his wings, and claim his vision
and see your life roads from his sky?

Everything is conspiring to show you
what heaven and earth want to happen.
When you think your way is lost,
when there are mountains of glass
and concrete between you and your dreams,

the ones who move beyond the curtain
of our consensual hallucinations
and speak as the wind in the trees
as the call of a bird, as the bark of a fox,
will open ways where you least expect them.
All you need are new ears and fresh eyes.

CHAPTER ONE

MAKING
REAL MAGIC

There is one common breathing, one common flow;
all things are in sympathy.

— HIPPOCRATES

We are embarking on a path of real magic. Real magic is the art of bringing gifts from another world into this world. We do this when we go dreaming and when we remember to bring something back. In dreaming, we go to other realities that may include places of guidance, initiation, challenge, adventure, healing. When we bring something back from these excursions, and take action in ordinary life to embody the guidance and energy we receive, that is a practice of real magic.

We go dreaming in the night. We do it quite spontaneously. We can do it by setting an intention for our nocturnal adventures. We can do it as lucid dreamers, awakened to the fact that we are dreaming and able to navigate the dreamlands consciously. We can do it in the way of the shaman, traveling intentionally, conscious and hyperaware, riding the drum to locales beyond the ordinary, and bringing back gifts.

We can also walk the roads of everyday life as conscious

1

dreamers, learning to recognize how the world is speaking to us in signs and symbols, and how a deeper order of events may reveal itself through the play of synchronicity. In night dreams and conscious excursions, we get out there; we go near or far into other orders of reality where the rules of linear time and Newtonian physics do not apply. Through synchronicity, powers of the deeper reality come poking and probing through the walls of our consensual hallucinations to bring us awake. Sometimes they work to confirm or encourage us in a certain line of action; sometimes they intercede to knock us back and discourage us from persisting in the worst of our errors.

Synchronicity is when the universe gets personal. Navigating by synchronicity is the dreamer's way of operating 24/7. Though the word *synchronicity* is a modern invention — Jung made it up because he noticed that people have a hard time talking about coincidence — the phenomenon has been recognized, and highly valued, from the most ancient times. The Greek philosopher Heraclitus maintained that the deepest order in our experienced universe is the effect of "a child playing with game pieces" in another reality. As the game pieces fall, we notice the reverberations, in the play of coincidence.

When we pay attention, we find that we are given signs by the world around us every day. Like a street sign, a synchronistic event may seem to say Stop or Go, Dead End or Fast Lane. Beyond these signs, we find ourselves moving in a field of symbolic resonance that not only reflects back our inner themes and preoccupations, but provides confirmation or course correction. A symbol is more than a sign: it brings together what we know with what we do not yet know.

Through the weaving of synchronicity, we are brought awake and alive to a hidden order of events, to the understory of our world and our lives. As in the scene in the movie *The Matrix* when the black cat crosses the room in the same way twice, riffs of co-incidence (for which I have coined the term *reincidence*) can teach us that consensual reality may be far less solid than we supposed.

This book provides roadside assistance for the conscious traveler in the dream of waking life. We will learn how the world is speaking to us in many voices through signs and symbols and synchronicity, and how we can bring from these many voices guidance, joy, and a deeper sense of what it is all about. This is a book of practice rather than theory, and I will follow the Gryphon's advice:

> "Explain all that," said the Mock Turtle.
> "No, no! The adventures first," said the Gryphon in an impatient tone: "explanations take such a dreadful time."
> [Lewis Carroll, *Alice's Adventures in Wonderland*]

Adventures are more fun than explanations, and a story is our easiest way to get to the truth of a matter and to carry that truth. I will start with three personal stories because I agree with Mark Twain when he says, "I do not wish to hear about the moon from someone who has not been there." These stories are not about traveling to the moon (I have written about that in other books), but about encounters with a deeper reality in quite ordinary places: a pub, a gritty urban street, and a backyard.

You do not need to travel far to encounter powers of the deeper world or to hear oracles speak. You are at the center of the multidimensional universe right now. The doors to the Otherworld open from wherever you are, and the traffic moves both ways.

A SEAT IN THE FOX'S PUB

The fox had put his name on the pub, which should have clued me in to the possibility that stopping here for a beer and a bite might be more than a routine affair. The Firkin and Fox. Thoroughly English sounding, but used on the American side of the big pond for a chain of airport restaurants that do not have English ales on tap, and where you probably will not find meat pies or bangers on the menu. It was the only sit-down place with alcohol available that seemed to be open on that long concourse at Washington's Dulles airport, so I was ready to take the best I could get.

There was already a tilt to my day, that shift away from the sense that the world is solid or fixed that comes when your plans have been screwed up and you are traveling on a completely different itinerary from the one you had had signed, sealed, and emailed. I had discovered in the early hours that the first flight in a long journey had been canceled. I had to wait only twenty minutes in a phone queue before a helpful agent rebooked me. I was now traveling via Dulles instead of Newark. So be it. Such changes in plans bring a Trickster energy into play. If you can avoid type A personality disorder and are not allergic to surprises, you may find things and people coming together in unusual ways, giving you, at the least, the gift of a fresh story.

However, it did not seem that the Firkin and Fox was going to be part of my story. The place was jam-packed.

I was moving on when a woman started disentangling herself from her seat at the bar. The young man next to her reached down to help her with her bags. As she came toward me, I moved to take her seat.

"Your timing is exquisite," I thanked her.

"You are going to enjoy that young man," was her unlikely response.

The young man at the bar was behaving oddly, hopping back and forth between the now vacant seat and the one he had been sitting on. He finally decided I could have his previous seat. Clearly, there was going to be some kind of engagement here. His baby-blue eyes floated up out of a pale and desperate face.

He declared, "I know you are an elder. I have been asking for an elder to help me."

He asked me to guess his age. I did, and got it right. Twenty-two. Now he was almost beseeching. "What can you tell me about life?"

"Never leave home without your sense of humor."

"I know. But I get so intense, so aggressive. Like, if someone bumps the back of my seat" — he thumped on the back of my seat to make his point — "I want to get up and get in that guy's face."

He hit the back of my seat a second time, but I did not lose my beer or my patience. "I'll tell you something else I have learned about life," I said carefully. "We always have the freedom to choose our attitude."

He stopped banging the back of my seat. "Oh my God, you're right. It's amazing you just sit down next to me and say that."

He pushed his face close to mine as if he needed to be petted. He reminded me of someone. Who was it? Got it. He resembled Sméagol in *The Lord of the Rings*, in his gentler, beseeching mode. The absence of hair on his head was the least notable point of resemblance.

He spoke of how he was headed for San Francisco, to make some new life. He knew nobody in the Bay Area. I assured him he would make friends soon enough, and gave him a few suggestions about the city.

He wanted something more from me I could not yet fathom.

As he went on talking, questioning, I began to sense the shape and the history of his need. He talked about his military family in Virginia and his estrangement from his father, who sounded like an iron-hard soldier of the old Southern school. He had suffered some recent shaming and rejection by his father, and he was bleeding inside. It took no great intuition on my part to realize that his dad had not been able to accept that this young man was gay.

I told him that I, too, came from a military family and that

I had been estranged from my father until three years before his death, when we became the best of friends. I told the young man that if it were my life, I would make it my game to make all well with my dad while he was still in the world.

"You're giving me goose bumps." He showed me. His whole arm was chicken skin.

"Truth comes with goose bumps."

He was crying now, leaking onto my shoulder.

"You come into the bar," he sobbed, "you take a seat, and you tell me the most important things I've ever been told."

"Here's something else I've learned: The world speaks to us through coincidence and chance encounters. It's a kind of magic."

"Is that what you are? A magician? You got me crying at the bar, for chrissake."

"Well that lady who gave me her seat did give you a good review."

I was ready to leave.

"Can I see you again?"

"No, this was our moment. The only time for us."

He wanted to pay for my burger and beer. Of course I would not let him.

"Can I at least have a hug?"

I gave him that.

As I headed for my departure gate, I turned back to look at the fox on the sign of the pub. I said in my mind, *Thank you.* I had the deep feeling that my chance encounter with the desperate young man at the bar had pulled him back from the brink of suicide. There is often more than chance going on in a chance encounter.

"HE CAN'T KILL US BOTH AT THE SAME TIME, CAN HE?"

One of the everyday oracles the Greeks valued most highly was the *kledon*. A kledon is sound or speech coming out of silence or undifferentiated noise. In the formless hubbub of a city street, I received a kledon one summer that gave me very direct guidance on a conflictive situation. It not only echoed the situation back to me in a way that enabled me to grasp its essence; it gave me an immediate and practical means to handle that tricky situation with tact and bring it to happy resolution.

A kledon is often something you overhear — a snatch from a stranger's conversation, a song from a passing car radio, the croak or cry of a bird, the siren of an ambulance. My kledon that day was pointed at me, inspired by my little dog, Oskar.

Oskar is a miniature schnauzer who weighs about twenty pounds. He has hosts of admirers. It is not unusual for him to draw three cries like "What a cutie!" in a single block. That morning, he drew a different kind of remark.

Walking Oskar toward the park around breakfast time, I was debating with myself whether I could really manage to take on two big new projects that season. Each project would demand a great amount of time, energy, and focus. Worse, it was possible that they could prove to be mutually competing and that I would find myself out of favor with both project managers.

I had not asked for specific guidance that morning. But I had the theme on my mind when a stranger got out of his truck a few houses up the street from my home. He hoisted a huge carton of stuff out of his vehicle, raising it to shoulder height. As he approached me, he pointed his chin at my dog and said, "He can't kill us both at the same time, can he?"

I was startled, slightly shaken. Instead of coming up with a riposte, which I am usually good at, I walked on, trying to make sense of this unexpected wisecrack. I felt that behind the joke, a Joker of a larger kind was in play.

I played with possible fits between the humorous question the stranger had addressed to me and the inner question that was on my mind. The inner question was, *Can I handle two new projects at the same time?* The kledon I received was, "He can't kill us both at the same time, can he?" It did not cause brain damage to figure out the connection. I had been told I could not tackle more than one project at a time.

I accepted the message. I could not "kill" two big projects at once. I would have to "kill" one of them in the sense of dropping it, in order to "kill" the other in the sense of successful execution. I knew which project I would now drop. Having made that choice, I needed to find the right way to communicate my decision to the very nice project manager I was about to disappoint.

I picked up the phone a couple of hours later. The project manager was unhappy when I told him I would have to bow out of plans made long before, especially when I explained that this was because I was choosing another company and another venture over his. The conversation was a little strained until I told him my dog story. When I repeated the kledon, "He can't kill us both at the same time," the manager roared with laughter. He shouted, "I get it!"

I thanked him and gave a nod to the Joker I sensed behind the joke on the street that day.

THE BOOK OF THE DEAD AND THE SQUIRREL OF MISCHIEF

The more grave the issue, the more important to keep our sense of humor. Death is much too serious to be approached with solemnity.

I was at home on a bitter winter's night, working feverishly on a book that became *The Dreamer's Book of the Dead*, when I felt that a mythic trickster came into play in the small, furry body of a backyard animal. I was up at 4:00 AM because I was determined that on this particular night I was somehow going to crack the Yeats Code. The great Irish poet William Butler Yeats made it one of the great quests of his life to deliver a grand modern myth, a Book of the Dead that would match the famous ones from Egypt and Tibet but speak in images and forms better suited to the contemporary world. With his immense power of poetic speech, Yeats had the voice to carry through his design. His lifelong dedication to *experiential* research into the realms of spirit and the spirits, his experiments in "mutual visioning," and his craft as a working magician of a great esoteric order gave him the raw materials for a Book of the Dead that would be founded on firsthand knowledge of the things that really matter.

But he exhausted himself, and his readers, with his efforts to pull it all together in prose in two versions of the book he called *A Vision*. I was determined, that night, to follow him as far as he was able to go. And come 4:00 in the morning, I had a headache and was utterly exhausted by the complex machinery of the last version of *A Vision* that he had published. While Yeats' poetry had thrilled and winged my imagination since boyhood, I felt that his attempt at a Book of the Dead (the part of *A Vision* that he titled "The Soul in Judgment") was actually cramping my mind and narrowing the gates of perception.

That winter, I was living, as well as working, in the basement apartment of my family home in a small Rust Belt city in the Northeast. I call this space my Cave. I staggered to the bedroom, dropping my clothes in a heap on the floor, and threw myself naked under the covers. I was on my way to dreamland when I heard a series of noises just behind my head. Scratching and scraping, then some rustling and scampering and — yes — some palpable gnawing.

Squirrels. I had been vaguely aware of their nesting activities around and under the back porch. Since the thermometer dropped into the single digits, they had been working to keep themselves warm and cozy, gathering old papers and leaves and garden trash into snugs and shanties under the back stairs. I had not felt any desire to interfere with their comforts — until now.

I was so very tired. Maybe if I pulled the covers up over my ears, I could ignore the noises from behind the wall.

I heard *scratch, rustle, BANG!* The last sound was *exactly* that of someone knocking.

My effort to ignore the squirrels was not prospering. Near the foot of the bed was a downstairs door to the garden, but we had not used it in years. I pulled a book table out of the way and struggled with the locks. When I finally got the door open, the squirrels fell silent. Naked, shivering against the deep snow in the yard, I snarled threats about what would happen to them if my sleep was disrupted again. I needed rest, and I also wanted dreams to ripen the words I was forming for things that were hard to express.

Scratch, rustle, scrape. Now one of the squirrels was running up and down the exterior wall of the house, inches from my head. I could picture him, fat and big and cocky, showing off to his harem and to lesser males in the pack, or whatever a collective of squirrels is called.

Knock, knock, BANG!

This was too much. Still naked, I wrenched open the door and yelled homicidal threats into the dark. Silence. Maybe the squirrels believed me this time. Back to bed.

Ratta-patta-tosk-BAM! Louder than before.

I pulled on my clothes and flung myself out the back door, into the snowy yard. I made snowballs and ice balls and threw them into the dark below the stairs. I found a hoe and poked and jabbed with that, at the litter under the back porch where the squirrel's nest must be.

Back inside my Cave, I listened for a while, calculating my next moves if the squirrels started their wild rumpus again. In my little world, there was now deep silence. But I was deep awake.

When in doubt, walk the dog. He had heard me stirring and

was doing a tap dance on the landing above the Cave, ready to go. We would make this quick and functional, a run to the Poop Park — the little neighborhood park just one block away — rather than the Big Park, a block further off on the other side. Weary as I was, I could not refrain from chuckling over the episode with the squirrels. This was surely a message to lighten up. I had been taking my work, in Yeats' cause, far too seriously for far too long. When I pictured the squirrel running up and down my back wall, I remembered that there is a squirrel in Nordic mythology who keeps running up and down the World Tree, Yggdrasil, causing no end of mischief. His name is Ratatosk, and you hear scamper and patter in the syllables of that name.

It was strange to encounter another dog walker in the Poop Park on that bitter night, still hours away from dawn. She was a redhead walking a redhead, a beautiful Irish setter. His name was Fergus. Of course. I started reciting the lines from Yeats:

For Fergus rules the brazen cars,
And rules the shadows of the wood,
And the white breast of the dim sea
And all disheveled wandering stars.

I realized I was performing a duet. Fergus' owner said the lines with me, half singing. Yes, she had named her dog for Yeats' poem "Who Goes with Fergus?"

The squirrel got me out of bed, and the poet walked with me.

Back in the Cave, I went back to writing. I wrote for hours, and the contractions of a new book coming through came faster and easier. When I lay down after lunch, I said, *Thank you*. I rose again later with tides of words moving within me, like lake water lapping, and wrote from this and found that my book was being born like a delivery in water, without pain.

Life rhymes. Ten years later, in identical weather, with the thermometer dipping below zero, I sat down at 4:00 AM and wrote up this story. Precisely at that moment, a squirrel at the front door started making a terrific racket among some garbage. This climaxed with a tremendous *BANG* as the squirrel succeeded in pulling down something very tall and heavy. Ratatosk in the backyard becomes Ratatosk of the sidewalk oracles.

◆

These little stories give a taste of what it is like when we meet the marvelous, or the weird, in everyday life. We know that this is a special moment. What is happening gives us shivers. We feel that the universe just got very personal. We sense that a hidden hand, or another mind, is at work. That encounter with the desperate man in the foxy pub happened by chance but felt like it came about through a *call*, from him or something watching over him. It was perfectly timed and choreographed, with the lady with the luggage getting up from *that* seat at *that* moment. The stranger with a heavy load who joked that my dog could not kill both of us at the same time helped me release myself from an impossibly heavy load I was about to take on. It felt as if some unseen power, a numen with a sense of humor, was using his vocal chords to provide counsel. The noisy squirrel who kept me awake and writing was trying to get warm on a wintry night. He also became a backyard Ratatosk, a properly proportioned avatar of a Trickster whose mischief keeps the worlds turning.

In the yard with the Squirrel of Mischief, in the park with Fergus of the "disheveled wandering stars," I felt I was on a mythic edge, the kind of edge that can sharpen you to live and tell bigger and bolder stories. I sensed that, because I had taken on a difficult challenge and was going at it full bore, I had drawn the interest of players behind the scenes. Take on greater tasks, and you draw the support of greater powers. Whatever we do feeds different spirits and attracts or repels different people and events. The law of attraction is always at play and is no secret to those who are awake in the conscious universe. In special moments, we notice that it is being played harder. We are all strange attractors, and there are moments when the magnetism we exert — or is exerted on us by others — is especially strong. When you are giving your best to an affair of the heart, be it a romance or a creative project or a cause, you draw the attention of greater powers. According to how you choose to use your gifts, you draw the support or the indifference of other intelligences.

Words matter. In the beginning was the Word, the Logos, we have been told. When the Ancestors walked this earth, Australian Aborigines say, they brought things into being by naming them. When Isis learns the secret name of Ra, she has power over the greatest of the gods. So we will spend a little time in the first chapter talking about *how we talk* about synchronicity, and how it is understood in wisdom traditions. I will offer a new word to describe the *practice* of navigating by synchronicity. The word is *kairomancy*. It combines the Greek words *kairos*, meaning a "special moment," and *manteia*, meaning "oracle" or "divination." Kairomancy (not to be confused with chiromancy!) is the art of divination through special moments, in the Kairos time of special opportunity that puts a thrill of possibility in your mind and body and can set your world trembling.

Kairos time is when you are released, if only for a moment, from the breakable laws of linear time and space, when things come to you, and you to them, by a different logic. In such marvelous moments, things may unfold in ways the new physics, as well as ancient shamans and seers, can recognize and for which contemporary science even has names, like "entanglement," or "retrokinesis," or "quantum effects on a macro scale."

Some of this science has been made more accessible to

nonscientific minds by the movie *Interstellar* and the book by Kip Thorne, the physicist who inspired some of that film's most gripping scenes and scenarios, *The Science of Interstellar*. There are scenes in the film where we see an astronaut who is dead or in the future (or both) trying to reach into 3-D reality from some dimension X, working to cause physical effects that will allow his message to reach his daughter (and save the world). With huge effort, pushing from a tesseract space, he shoves a book forward on a bookcase and writes four letters in dust. Later he installs a code in a wristwatch that can be read through the second hand.

In the play of synchronicity, we encounter similar phenomena. Any book lover is familiar with the behavior of shelf elves, who seem to push books out of bookcases and make them appear or disappear. I was first invited to lead a workshop on shamanic dreaming in Madison, Wisconsin, because a well-known shamanic practitioner from that creative oasis walked into a bookstore in another state, looking for something else. A copy of my book *Conscious Dreaming* flew off a shelf and hit him in the middle of the forehead, over the third eye. He had never heard of me, and the book — the first of the many I have written on the many ways of dreaming — had just been published. He honored the spirits of synchronicity by purchasing the book. When he read it, he decided that the marriage of shamanism and dreamwork I had solemnized without a shotgun was so important that he wanted me to bring it to his town.

Since watching the tesseract scene in *Interstellar*, I wonder whether shelf elves are sometimes humans who are able to reach from the future or the afterlife and "tesser" in on us. I have personal experience of what I believe to be interventions by a future self that have been vital correctives in my life. In Kairos moments, we may discern interweavings of energy presences from different realities and the crisscrossing of event tracks from parallel worlds.

Wilder stories and speculations lie ahead, especially in the last chapters of this book. Yet chances are you will find that any part of this book is where the wild things are. When we make synchronicity our theme, we bring the Trickster into play. His presence was in the opening story, the light brush of the fox's tale. It became louder in the *rat-tat-tosk* of the Squirrel of Mischief. We will meet him again and again in these pages until he and his Fox avatar insist on their own chapter.

You will hear more from poets than physicists in these pages. This does not mean that this book is devoid of a science of synchronicity. It offers *applied* science: how to read and navigate signs, symbols, and synchronicity in everyday life. It does not attempt to offer a scientific *theory* of how these things work, though we will draw from both ancient and modern models of understanding. We are less interested in how and why these things work than that they *do* work, and offer a rich harvest if we work — or rather, play — with them.

Here's where the poets come in. If you want to become a *kairomancer* — one who practices the applied science of synchronicity — you need a poet in your soul. Why? Because navigating by synchronicity requires you to grow your ability to recognize what rhymes in a day, or a week, or a life. It demands, and grows, that "talent for resemblances" that was held to be the primary requirement for a dream interpreter in ancient Greece.

Sidewalk Oracles is, above all, a book of games. Chapter 4 is full of them. The games invite you to *come to your senses*, to come fully awake and alive in both your bodily senses and your inner senses. They encourage you to receive whatever enters your field of perception as a personal message from the animate universe about your present condition. You will find yourself challenged to *check your attitude* and notice how your attitude is forever strutting or stumbling or moping in front of you, preparing the events and encounters that will suit it perfectly. You will not find magic in your world unless you carry magic within you. *Sidewalk Oracles* invites you to treat every day as a play day and an opportunity to make real magic.

In composing this book, I found myself cutting through jungles of complexity, untangling strangler vines and coaching pythons to speak and perform, in the effort to open a simple path that can take you beyond previous maps and familiar fields. This path will never be straight, not in the territories we are entering here. Gorgeous hybrids, flying fish, and great felines with golden eyes will prowl at the jungle edge and shimmer overhead. But I have tried to make the path clear and simple, with fresh signage — so simple that when you choose to walk it, you may wish that you had found it decades ago, or feel that you have been walking it all your life, in your dreams, even though it did not exist until Now.

CHAPTER TWO

A WALK AROUND
JUNG'S TOWER

*The layman always means, when he says "reality,"
that he is speaking of something self-evidently known;
whereas to me it seems the most important and exceedingly
difficult task of our time is to work
on the construction of a new idea of reality.*

— WOLFGANG PAULI, LETTER TO MARKUS FIERZ,
AUGUST 12, 1948

Meaningful coincidence has to do with the intersection of timeless forces with the world of time, with the "understory" beneath and behind the surface events of our lives irrupting into our field of perception. This most certainly produces synchronous experiences. But it can also generate "rhyming" sequences played out, in dream and in waking, over days, weeks, or years.

Synchronicity may stop our breath. In a Kairos moment, the world stops, too, and it opens.

Detectives say "it's not coincidence" when they are pursuing clues to a case. "Do you know what we call coincidences in my profession?" asks Inspector Ayala, the detective in *Gran Hotel*, a popular Spanish *telenovela*. "Suspicions!" A detective might well conclude that it is no coincidence that two suspects fly from opposite sides of the world to check in to a hotel in the Bahamas on the same day. He will presume that there is an arrangement, a tryst, a secret plot.

Jung said, "It is not coincidence," when a steel knife exploded in a locked cabinet in his family home. He was twenty-three, a graduate student, out in the garden at the time. He heard a sound like a pistol shot and rushed inside to find his elderly mother confused and shaken. They searched for the source of the explosion and eventually found that a steel bread knife had shattered into four pieces, which were lying inside a breadbasket next to a loaf of bread. The basket and the bread were untouched. "The explosive force apparently did not exceed that amount of energy which was just needed to break the knife and was completely exhausted with the breaking itself," Jung later reported to the parapsychologist J. B. Rhine.

The next day, Jung took the knife to a master cutler, who examined it under a magnifying glass and told him that there was no flaw in the metal. The knife could only have been broken by deliberate human action. "Someone has been pulling your leg." This was physically impossible.

The incident was part of a pattern. Within a few days, a similar bang like a pistol shot was heard in the house. This time the source was an exploding table. The top of a solid round table cracked from the rim to beyond the center.

Jung was certain these incidents could not be ascribed to chance. There had to be some hidden force at work. Playing holistic detective, he decided the explosions were connected to the explosive emotions that had been stirred by his experiments with his psychic cousin "Helly" Preiswerk. They had conducted séances together since they were teenagers but had recently stopped. Jung concluded that the explosions were a signal to resume the experiments. Though things eventually went sour, he later declared that the period of the séances with Helly contained "the origin of all my ideas."

Jung came to describe synchronicity as "an acausal connecting principle." But the connection between a charged psychic atmosphere and poltergeist-like phenomena — repeated in Jung's relations with Freud prior to their breakup — does not seem to be void of causation. There was no physical hand on the knife, but it felt like some hidden hand was at work; and this is what we often feel when synchronicity strikes. Synchronicity may be wild, but perhaps it is never truly random.

YOU KNOW IT WHEN YOU FEEL IT

It's a rule of skin: truth comes with goose bumps (or chicken skin, if you like). There is a science of shivers, which involves learning to recognize and respect what is going on when something exceptional is in the air and your body responds even before your mind can make sense of it. For the ancients, and in shamanic traditions, trembling for reasons other than cold or external danger has always been regarded as a sign of the advent of the numinous, the coming of gods or spirits.

> We always lose the essential. That's the law
> when we try to speak about the numen.
> [Jorge Luis Borges, "The Moon"]

Borges, with poetic clarity, is telling us how hard it is to define an experience of the marvelous, or to give it the right name. As a lover of Virgil and the classics, he falls back on the Roman word *numen*. It's a good one, and it speaks to us about what we often feel in play when we encounter meaningful coincidence.

The word *numen* literally means a "nod." It comes to mean the presence or blessing of a sacred power, a nod from on high. Cicero used the word to mean the "active power" of a deity. Residents of Colorado should know something about this because the state motto is "Nil sine numine," for which a literal translation would be "nothing without a divine nod." The motto is a contraction of a line from Virgil's *Aeneid*: "non haec sine numine devum eveniunt" (these things do not come to pass without a nod from above).

The German scholar of religion Rudolf Otto gave us the adjective *numinous*. Otto's Prussian appearance — Kaiser mustache, high-collared tunic, ramrod bearing — belied his deep interest in mystical experience. His classic work *The Idea of the Holy* greatly influenced Jung and homes in on something central to our efforts to understand how to recognize and talk about situations where we feel the presence of something that has come from above — or below or behind — the structures of ordinary reality. Otto observed that we can only grasp the nature of the numinous through our feelings. The numinous "cannot, strictly speaking, be taught, it can only be evoked, awakened in the mind; as everything that comes 'of the spirit' must be awakened." He informs us that "the numinous is felt as objective and outside the self." The feelings aroused are of mystery, often reinforced by "shudders." Feelings may span the spectrum from "a gentle tide" to a sudden eruption with spasms and convulsions, to "the strangest excitements," "wild and demonic forms," or "hushed, trembling and speechless humility of the creature."

On the roads of everyday life, we are more likely to talk — or try to talk — about "coincidence" or "synchronicity" than about the presence of a numen. But Otto was absolutely right about one thing. When you encounter the numinous, by any name, you will know it by what you *feel*. You feel it in your fingers, in your toes, and especially in your skin. It is, first and last, through our feelings that we know that coincidence is going on, and that it is meaningful. It can tickle, or punch you in the gut. It can stop your breath or make you jump with delight. It can give you cold chills or warm shivers. It can feel like a pat on the shoulder, like a *bisou* on your cheek, like a jab in the small of your back.

Feeling is your clue to meaning. I made an informal survey of eight hundred people who follow my work. I asked them the following question: When you encounter significant coincidence (a.k.a. synchronicity), what do you feel, and what do you say about it?

Here are some of the responses:

- "Usually, I say, 'Bring it on!' I feel I am being shown I am on the right path."
- "I say thank you. I feel motivated to be alert and to be present."
- "I shudder. I feel a tilt in the world. I say, 'Hot damn!'"
- "For a moment, the whole world stops, and I am at one with the universe."
- "I always feel deeply grateful and special. Sometimes I giggle; sometimes I feel awe and oneness. The biggies I share with those who may appreciate or gain from it, and I try to note them all in my gratitude journal to keep 'em coming."
- "I feel lucky and supported and connected, and I tell other people, to remind them of the story that we are collectively woven into."
- "Laughing and expectant, I say, 'Yes!' and 'Thank you!'"
- "I get the warm fuzzy feeling like the universe is allowing me to see a few of the strings behind the special effects."
- "It's like waking up suddenly."
- "I feel I'm on the right path, in touch, connected."

- "I feel like I'm being nagged by something with a peculiar sense of humor. I generally chuckle and say, 'All right then.'"
- "The message for me is, Pay attention."
- "I say, 'Ah...someone is listening after all.'"
- "I say thank you to the universe and spirit, and then I always wonder what I might have been missing when I wasn't noticing a synchronicity around me."
- "I say, 'Gimme more please!' 'Thank you!' and 'What can I do with this?' It makes me feel alive, enchanted, and the world becomes sharper."

What is most striking in this informal survey is that no one described the experience of synchronicity as scary. They find it thrilling and exciting. They did not speak of synchronicity as strange, either in the sense of being foreign to normal experience or in the sense of being a rare phenomenon in their lives. On the contrary, they spoke again and again of how the experience makes them feel at home in a conscious, benign universe where they are recognized and supported. Some talked of receiving "divine winks" or "secret handshakes."

Nobody described the experience of synchronicity as "weird" until I introduced focused discussion of that word later on. Again and again, I heard responders saying, "Gimme more please" and "Bring it on!" What was "weird" to them was not the phenomenon of synchronicity, but missing out on it.

THE STONE JUNG'S BUILDERS REJECTED

Jung dreamed of a tower and he built it, on old church land at the edge of the village of Bollingen, on the shore of the Obersee basin of Lake Zurich. He started work soon after his mother's death in 1923. What began as a simple neo-medieval tower with a pointed roof grew, in successive waves of inspiration and construction, into a small castle. Jung embarked on the final phase of construction after his wife Emma's death in 1955, adding a high upper room he called "the chapel" to the middle building between what were now two towers. He painted the walls with scenes of other times and filled the room with things that took him "out of time, out of the present."

He always refused to install electricity and indoor plumbing. He lived here like a farmer of an earlier time, pumping his own water, chopping wood for his fire, lighting his candles and oil lamps, cooking his hearty stews. He spent several months of the year at Bollingen. He came for solitude and simplicity, leaving behind his patients, his lecture room audiences, and his persona as professor and professional analyst. He went about in old, comfortable clothes and was often to be seen in overalls and even, on occasion, washing a pair of jeans. He did the best of his creative writing here in the last period of his life.

Very often, if you were nearby, you could hear the tap of Jung's chisel or the clang of his hammer. He worked here with stone as well as paper, covering many surfaces with images and inscriptions. He called the whole place his "confession in stone." Some of the things he carved are there for any visitor to see; some are hidden. One of the hidden inscriptions reads, in Latin, *Philemonis sacrum Faust poenetentia* [*sic*], which means "sanctuary of Philemon, penitence of Faust." Philemon was the name by which Jung knew the spiritual guide whose importance is fully revealed in the Red Book, the guide who, as he wrote, convinced him of the objective reality of the psyche and its productions. Philemon is also the name, in the myth, of a kindly old man who gives hospitality to gods who are traveling in disguise — and is killed, together with his gentle wife, through the greed and megalomania of Faust, the model of heedless Western man, in part 2 of Goethe's *Faust*.

When he was writing his essay on synchronicity, Jung carved the face of a laughing Trickster on the west wall of the original tower.

Jung's confession in stone contains many images that spark fire in the imagination but do not immediately yield explanation, except where Jung has added words, always in Greek or Latin, which he read fluently. Here is a woman reaching for the udder of a mare. Here is a bear behind her, apparently rolling a ball. Here is Salome. Here is a family crest.

The best story of Jung's stonework involves the block that was not supposed to be delivered. Jung wanted to build a wall for his garden. He engaged a mason who gave exact measurements for the stones required to the owner of a quarry while Jung was standing by. The stones were delivered by boat. When unloaded, it was clear at once that there had been a major mistake. The cornerstone was not triangular, as ordered. It was a perfect cube of much larger dimensions, about twenty inches thick. Enraged, the mason ordered the workmen to reload this block on the boat. Jung intervened, saying, "That is my stone! I must have it." He knew at once that the stone his mason had rejected would suit him perfectly for a purpose he did not yet understand.

Fairly soon, he decided to chisel a quotation from one of his beloved alchemists on one side of the cube. But something deeper was stirring, through affinity between Jung and the stone itself. On a second face of the stone, he saw something like a tiny eye, looking at him. He chiseled a definite eye. Around it he carved the shape of a little hooded figure, a homunculus. He had a name for this figure, Telesphoros. The name means "one who guides to completion." In Greek mythology, he is a son of Asklepios, the patron of dream healing. This figure was a recurring archetype in Jung's inner life, one he sought to give physical form with pen and chisel and, as a boy, with a pocket knife. When he was ten years old, Jung carved a little manikin of this kind from a school ruler and kept it hidden in a box. He regarded this as his first great secret in life, and "the climax and conclusion" of his childhood.

Now, around Telesphoros, he chiseled words in Greek that came to him. In *Memories, Dreams, Reflections* they are translated as follows: "Time is a child — playing like a child — playing a board game — the kingdom of the child. This is Telesphoros, who roams through the dark regions of this cosmos and glows like a star out of the depths. He points the way to the gates of the sun and to the land of dreams." The broken first sentence is a loose translation of one of the most mysterious and compelling fragments of the ancient Greek philosopher Heraclitus. Key words are open to rival translations. The word Jung renders as "time" is *aion*, and that is perhaps not a strong enough rendering. A recent translation of the line from Heraclitus offers this: "Lifetime is a child at play, moving pieces on a board. Kingship belongs to the child."

I wonder whether Jung played with the idea, as he chiseled, that what Heraclitus was talking about was a secret law of manifestation, perhaps none other than what Jung dubbed synchronicity. Beyond logic, beyond causation as it is commonly understood, the play of forces outside time determines what happens within the human experience of time. Play is what we must be most serious about. Play in the spirit of the child, who plays without concern for consequences, because *the play is the thing*.

So: "*Synchronicity* is a child at play, moving pieces on a board." On our side of reality, we see the pieces move, but not the hand that moves them.

Jung once said that he could bear the thought of being reincarnated back into this world if he could have Bollingen again.

Toward the end of his life, however, he knew for sure that there was a second Bollingen, ready for him on the other side. He dreamed that he saw the other Bollingen bathed in a glow of light. A voice told him that it was now completed and ready for him to move in. Far below its towers, he saw a mother wolverine in the water, teaching her kit to dive and swim.

Jung told this dream to two women, both analysts, who were close to him and had chosen to carry on his legacy. He was nearing eighty-five, his once robust health and energy were variable, and he had lost his "two wives," Emma and Toni Wolff. Jung and his confidants understood that the dream of the other Bollingen was making him familiar with death, showing him that he had a beautiful place to go on the other side and preparing him to enter a new phase of learning that would include operating in a new element, like the wolverine's child in the water. After the dream, Jung no longer felt the urgent need to return to Bollingen that had often gripped him. He stayed away for many weeks at a time before leaving for the other Bollingen nine months after the dream.

Synchronicity crackled around Jung's death, as he had suggested that it often does around the great turns in a life cycle. The last time he was out for a leisurely drive, he was held up by *three* wedding convoys, sowing thoughts of "three weddings and a funeral" decades before the film. Half an hour before she received the news of his death, his acolyte Barbara Hannah found that her car battery was inexplicably dead. An hour after Jung's death, lightning struck a tall poplar at the lakeside edge of his garden, stripping the bark and spreading it all over his lawn.

A few months before Jung's death, Gerhard Adler watched him as he sat at his desk in the "chapel" at Bollingen, looking out over the lake "but clearly looking out very much further and deeper. He sat, completely unaware of my presence, intensely still and absolutely concentrated, utterly alone with himself and engrossed in his inner images — the picture of a sage completely absorbed in a world of his own."

◆

Jung only carved three of the faces of the cornerstone the mason rejected. But he divided the Greek inscription around the hooded boy into four quarters, making a mandala. Jung loved what was foursquare, solid, a quaternity.

So starting from here, at Bollingen, let us look to the four directions for ways to understand synchronicity and for words to describe it from four ancient and primal traditions. Jung, the universal scholar and tireless mental and physical traveler, studied all of these traditions but did not make their vocabulary his own, preferring to cleave to the classics and his ability to spin new words out of old Greek and Latin. This was a man, after all, who would relax in the evening with a Latin tome when not reading a detective story.

We will start by traveling east, to the China of the Tao and the *Book of Changes*. Then south, to the Australia of the Dreaming and the Speaking Land. Then west to the Native American understanding of Orenda and All Our Relations. And finally north, to the Norse-German realms of Wyrd and weirder, which Jung found so problematic.

THE WAY AND THE CHANGES

Looking east from Jung's tower, we find in China a word and a way of understanding that are simple and profound. The word is *Tao* (also transliterated as *Dao*). It is sometimes translated as "way," or "*the* Way," which is good enough for me. If we are attuned to the Tao, then our ways are open.

The Tao of Psychology, Jean Shinoda Bolen's lively little book from 1979, is one of the very best expositions of the theory of synchronicity. She goes looking for an easier and more elegant way to explain the phenomenon Jung struggled to define. She found it waiting where it has been for thousands of years, in the Chinese understanding of the Tao, the Way that has no name but generates the ten thousand names.

> The Tao that can be told is not the eternal Tao
> The name that can be named is not the eternal name.
> The nameless is the beginning of heaven and earth
> The named is the mother of the ten thousand things.
> [Lao-tzu, *Tao Te Ching* (trans. Gia-Fu Feng and Jane English)]

As Bolen observed, "The Eastern mind has considered the underlying connection between ourselves and others, between ourselves and the universe, the essential reality and called it Tao." The *Book of Changes*, or *I Ching*, contains a method of invoking the Tao and is sometimes used as a divination system. Richard Wilhelm, who provided the first translation that made the Chinese oracle accessible for Western readers, decided that the best one-word rendering of *Tao* is "meaning."

Jung's thinking about synchronicity flowered when Richard Wilhelm sent him the text of an ancient Taoist treatise, *The Secret of the Golden Flower*, for which Jung wrote a preface. Wilhelm also introduced Jung to the *I Ching*. Jung studied the *I Ching* closely and realized he was entering the mind of a culture for which synchronicity — as the Way and its Changes — was the fundamental law of life and the preferred way of understanding what *wants* to happen in life.

The dynamic interplay between yin and yang is at the heart of the *I Ching*. It is the interplay between the receiving and the creating forces, between dark and light, between cool and warm, forever intermingled and turning into each other.

The emergence of the *I Ching* is wrapped in legend and mystery. By tradition, it was the ancient Dragon Emperor, Fu Xi, who "noticed" patterns in the cracks of turtle shells and distinguished these patterns as the eight trigrams (*pa kua*) that are the root of the *I Ching*. Later, the "King of Writing," Wu Wen, amplified the system into the sixty-four hexagrams, and Confucius ordered and numbered the arrangement.

Archaeology suggests an evolution over some four thousand years. Under the Shang dynasty, shamans read auguries in the cracks that appeared in the bones of animals offered as burned offerings. It was believed that as the appeals of humans traveled upward in the smoke, messages and warnings from higher powers came down. The relation between patterns of cracks and subsequent events was noted, and cracked bones were kept in preliterate "archives." Later, turtle shells were substituted. They provided a larger surface, and their shape was thought to resemble the dome of heaven above and the square fields of earth below. With the coming of the Bronze Age, turtle shells were cracked with bronze pokers. Patterns corresponding to later events began to be marked with simple symbols, suggesting fire or flood. From these symbols, Chinese writing emerged. Under the Chou dynasty — before the supply of turtles was exhausted — shamans and diviners began to record the code of the *I Ching* on strips of bamboo, tied together with silk ribbons. And the first books of China emerged.

The ancient method for casting the *I Ching* involves a fistful of dried yarrow stalks. The yarrow most valued for early divination was found growing on the graves of past teachers and masters of the *I Ching*, including Confucius. Early translator James Legge reported seeing yarrow growing on the grave of Confucius. The Chinese still believe that when a good diviner in the right state

of mind is doing his or her stuff, there is communication with
the spirits, whether you are using yarrow stalks or coins or grains
of rice, which my first teacher recommended, after lighting some
incense.

The *Great Treatise* (one of the earliest long commentaries on
the *I Ching*) maintains that the *I Ching* contains "the measure of
heaven and earth" — that is, it is a microcosm of the whole cosmic game — and that if we place ourselves in exactly the right
point in its revolutions, we move in synchrony with the workings
of the universe and can help shape events on every scale through
our conscious participation. The *Great Treatise* suggests that you
not only can learn to meet every event in the right way, but may
be privileged "to aid the gods in governing the world."

The *I Ching* hexagrams are stacks of six lines, broken or unbroken, variations on a single binary code. The unbroken lines
are *yang*; the broken ones are *yin*. Through this binary code, the
Book of Changes reveals the interplay of three realms: the earthly,
the human, and the heavenly. The two lowest lines of the hexagram relate to the Earth realm, the middle lines to the human, and
the upper pair to Heaven.

You don't use the *I Ching* for fortune-telling. It's not about
seeing the future; it's about seeing when and how to manifest your
hopes and plans for the future, which is actually much more interesting. This is a tool for helping you *create* the future you *choose*.
You bring your clear intention — your project — and you ask for
guidance on current conditions and the strategy to be followed.
The *I Ching* does not bind you to any determinist scheme of
things. It gives you a diagnosis of how things are, with the world
and with you *now*, whether this is the right time to pursue a goal,
and what strategy you should follow.

Since Jung's death, we have gained access to a manuscript of
the *Book of Changes* that is more ancient than those available in his

lifetime. It is a broken text and therefore not usable — without creative addition or fabrication — as a full oracle. Nonetheless, it makes very exciting reading for those interested in the shamanic origins of the oracle and the different levels on which it registers and provokes synchronicity.

The text dates from about 175 BCE. It was discovered in the tomb of a duke of the Han dynasty at Mawangdui that also contained the text of the *Tao Te Ching*, clearly placing this version of the Changes in the ancient Way. The ordering of the hexagrams in the Mawangdui version is quite different from that of the familiar Duke Wen arrangement used by Wilhelm and other translators. The two primal hexagrams have different and sexier names. Among the "appended statements" to the text, in Edward Shaughnessy's translation, we find this:

> The sage . . . takes the real characteristics of all under heaven to their extremes and causes them to reside in the hexagrams; *drums* the movements of all under heaven and causes them to reside in the statements; transforms and regulates them and causes them to reside in the alternations; pushes and puts them into motion and causes them to reside in the unity; makes them spiritual and transforms them and causes them to reside in his person; and plans and completes them . . . and causes them to reside in virtuous action.

Inspired by this, when I led a course in the *I Ching*, we *drummed* the binary code of the lines, changing and constant, yin and yang, on our single-headed frame drums and pictured early diviners doing something similar.

We drummed the six lines of the twentieth hexagram, which is called Watching and whose shape is that of a watchtower, the kind that Chinese armies placed along the borders. We saw how rising up through the lines of the hexagram is like climbing steps from the lowest level of an observation tower to the very top, from a place of limited or impeded vision to a space from which we could see, without restriction, across time and space.

A great revelation came when we worked, with drumming and also with body movements, with the sixty-first hexagram, called Zhong Fu (Wind on the Lake), or Inner Truth. The hole in the center of the hexagram can be seen as the opening of the heart, and also as the unveiling of a window between worlds. In Philip K. Dick's fascinating novel of alternate realities, *The Man in the High Castle*, the casting of this hexagram brings a shift between parallel worlds. In the main narrative, we are in a world where the Axis powers were the victors in World War II, and North America is divided between Japanese and German occupation armies and other entities. Yet a subversive work of fantasy is circulating, a story in which the Allies won the war and everything is different. When Juliana casts Zhong Fu for Abendsen in the last pages of *The Man in the High Castle*, he understands (if only for a moment) that the alternate reality he thought was fiction is true, the real world. We see the observer effect working on a human, and even global, scale. The act of observation changes what is being observed. If only for a shimmering moment, as the coins roll and settle, we glimpse how it may be possible to switch worlds.

The way we see reality generates our experience of reality. A method of observation like the *I Ching* can make us cocreators of our worlds. The *Great Treatise* suggests that through deep study of the *Book of Changes*, we not only learn to meet every event in the right way, but may be privileged "to aid the gods in governing the world." The Mawangdui text asserts that the *Book of Changes* "knows the reasons for light and dark." It "strengthens beings and fixes fate, taking pleasure in the way of all under heaven.... This is why the sage uses it to penetrate the will of all under heaven."

SPEAKING LAND

Look south, and we hear the First Peoples of Australia talking of the Speaking Land. Those who can hear the inner songs of the land can cross a thousand miles of desert without maps. "Nothing is nothing," they say in the Cape York Peninsula. Everything speaks of something else, and to something else. The spirit world and the physical world are interfused. The distance between them is the width of an eyelid, and no distance at all if the *strong* eye is open.

You know when it is the right time to do something by listening to the land, by recognizing those things that like to happen together. The Yolngu of the Northern Territory know when food is ready to be gathered in certain places because they notice things that like to happen at the same time. When a flower blooms in one place, you know it is time to harvest in another. When that tree blossoms, you know the yams in another spot are ripe and ready to eat. You do not check the calendar for the date of that big initiation ceremony; you know it's about time when a certain fish is jumping in the river, big and fat.

You grow in wisdom and the skills of survival by listening more and more closely to the Speaking Land. Your totem — which is not a symbol, but one of your most important selves — will help you. Suppose your totem animal is a sand goanna, a gnarly kind of lizard. Your elders will encourage you to watch the goanna as closely as you can while it hunts and hides, buries itself in a sand hill and comes out again. As you follow its life cycle, you develop a kinship connection with everything that shares the goanna's sand hill, with insects and birds, with plants and other animals, with the wind that tells the goanna when to dive into the sand and when to come up again.

Young girls of the Nhunggabarra in northern New South Wales were taken to a water hole for classes with the land. They stayed there for as long as three months, observing the behavior of the red dragonfly. From this patient and intimate connection with one small flying creature, they were expected to learn the cycle of life.

You learn that the birds are a whole telephone system. Night-hunting birds, like owls and frogmouths, are powerful spirits whose call can mean that someone close to you is about to die. Listen carefully to the kingfisher, who lent wings to Jung's Philemon. Kingfisher can see ghosts. If it calls out *ekwe, ekwe, ekwe*, watch out for a ghost attack that could inflict illness or even death. Little willie wagtail is a shaman of shamans among the bird tribes. He dances like an initiate in ceremony when he jitters sideways. Watch willie wagtail for any unusual behavior because this means news is coming. "Him good telephone that fella," a Ngarrindjeri woman of the lower Murray River told Philip Clarke, who has been helping to map the Aboriginal landscape.

Listen to water as well as earth, to the voices in a billabong, to the song of a river. Today the indigenous fishermen of the Torres Islands see and feel the "scars on the water" caused by boat propellers and pollutants. Their shaman, the *zogo le*, flies on the wings of a sea eagle and sees with its keen eyes.

Aborigines speak of a *seed power* that lives in the land. Whatever is enacted in a certain place leaves "a vibrational residue," Robert Lawlor tells us, "as plants leave an image of themselves as seeds." The shapes of the land, and its deepest vibrations, are the legacy of the Ancestors, who walked the earth in the creation time, the Dreaming. (We'll speak of them with a capital *A* to make clear they are more than previous generations of our biological families.) The seed power of each place is the Dreaming of that place, within the greater Dreaming or Dreamtime. "Everything in the natural world is a symbolic footprint of the metaphysical beings whose actions created our world. As with a seed, the potency of an earthly location is wedded to the memory of its origin."

The terms *the Dreaming* and *Dreamtime* derive from the early anthropology of Spencer and Gillen, who translated *Alcheringa* (which literally means "belonging to the dream") as "Dream Times," in order to distinguish a primordial creative time of the Ancestors from contemporary dreaming. The distinction is not made in the indigenous mind. The Ancestors are present and accessible *now* through dreaming. All that is required is to open the inner senses.

Let's be clear: there is the Dreaming, or the Dreamtime, the realm of gods and ancestral beings, and then there are personal dreams. The two interweave but are not the same. The Kukatja, in common with many other Western Desert tribes, use the word *Tjukurrpa* for the ancestral Dreaming but a different term — *kapukurri* — for personal dream experiences. Anthropologist Sylvie Poirier, who spent many years with the Kukatja, writes that "in Aboriginal Australia, dreams are the privileged space-time of communication between humans and ancestral beings, as between humans and spirits of the dead." Dreaming is active, not merely passive. It is a form of engagement. You can decide where you are going to go, and you can go consciously. Dreaming is soul travel. A dream is what happens when an aspect of the soul leaves the body and has encounters and adventures. "The spirit goes on walkabout," a Kukatja grandmother explains.

Your private dreams may not be truly private. You get out and about; you meet other people and other beings. You may even manage to travel into the Dreamtime, the World Up Top, the All-at-Once of the Ancestors.

You can also get there as you follow the tracks of the world around you, because the Dreaming is the bigger story that not only happened back then, in creation time, but is always going on. Dreamtime is not separate from the physical world. It is the inner pulse of the land.

In Dreamtime, the Ancestor spirits came to earth in human

and other forms. Other cultures might call such beings gods, but in the Aboriginal telling, they are simply the Ancestors. As they walk this Earth, the Ancestors mark it and shape it and bring things into being. These great ones are not confined to any earthly forms. They can be bird and snake and fish and human all at once. They are superhuman but have passions and jealousies and conflicts like humans — except even more. They fight, they have sex, they are endlessly fallible.

Where they crossed the earth, or fought or made love or rested, they created rivers and hills and other features of the land. That riverbed twists like that because a Bull Eel was trying to evade a Tiger Cat that was a very good fisherman. When you hear a story like this told, you think you are back in the infancy of the world, until you are able to hear it on its deeper levels. But even if you have access only to the outer layer of the story — the adventure, or sex drama, or just-so animal fable with no obvious moral — it will help you grow a personal connection with the land and help you hear the voices of the land.

Where the Dreaming tracks of many Ancestors converge or cross each other, as at Uluru in the desert heart of the continent, we have a place of exceptional potency.

The Ancestors left behind them "a world full of signs of their beneficent intent" toward human beings, according to W. E. H. Stanner. "The land might look brown and empty to other eyes, but is really like a great cathedral in which most of the choir and furniture of heaven and earth are regarded by the Aborigines as a vast sign system." When you are of this mind, you move "not in a landscape, but in a humanized realm saturated with significance."

◆

In Aboriginal English, a widespread synonym of Dreaming is "Law," in the sense of a body of spiritual and traditional knowledge, coded in stories, that helps you find patterns of connection and follow the Dreaming tracks.

For the Nhunggabarra, Earth is the mirror of the sky world, the tangible manifestation of an intangible world. Everything in the Speaking Land — that spider, that rock, that gum tree — has an ordinary and nonordinary aspect.

The Dreaming is *everywhen*. When it is with you, and you are with it, you know this in your inner and outer senses.

You understand synchronicity by doing it. You grow strong in this by developing what people in the Kimberley ranges call *kurara*, the ability to "talk to the land." You know that your own dreams can open the gates of the Dreamtime and that everywhere spirits are talking, talking.

ORENDA AND THE PRACTICE OF GIVING THANKS

Look west from Jung's tower, and we find the *orenda* of the Longhouse People of woodland America, who were dubbed "Iroquois" by the French, a name that has stuck. Orenda is the power that is in everything and beyond everything. It clusters in certain things — in that tree, in that stone, in that person or gathering — and if you are sensitive, you will feel its weight and its force.

People come from another world — in the Iroquoian cosmogony, they call it Earth-in-the-Sky — and the origin and purpose of life here below is to be found in that Sky World. "Tohsa sasa nikon'hren," they say. "Do not let your mind fall" from the memory of that other world where everything is directed and created by the power of thought and everything lives in the glow of a great Tree of Light.

The first person on Earth who was anything like a human came from that Sky World, after she fell — or was pushed — through a hole among the roots of its great tree. As she fell, she was caught on the wings of great blue herons, who carried her gently down to a chaos of water. Animals, diving into the black deep, found earth for her, so she could begin to make a world. Turtle offered its great back, and First Woman danced a new world into being. Under her feet, a handful of soil became all the lands we live on.

The memory of Earth-in-the-Sky in no way blurs the knowledge that orenda — which is power, spirit, energy, consciousness all at once — is in everything. In the way of the Onkwehonwe, the Real People (as the Iroquois call themselves), we must remember that our relations with our environment are entirely personal and require appropriate manners. If you want to take something from the Earth, you must ask permission. The hunter asks the spirit of the deer for permission to take its life and wastes nothing from its body. I once watched a Mohawk medicine man gathering healing plants. He started by identifying the elder among a stand of the plants and speaking to this one, seeking permission. He offered a little pinch of native tobacco in return for the stalks he gathered for medicine.

In this tradition, the best form of prayer is to give thanks for the gifts of life. In the long version of the Iroquois thanksgiving, you thank everything that supports your life, and as you do this, you announce that you are talking to family.

I give thanks to my brothers the Thunderers
I give thanks to Grandmother Moon and to Elder Brother
    Sun

If you have something to get off your chest, you might take a walk in the woods, not like a duck (as white people walk) but more like a pigeon, toes turned slightly inward to stop you from tripping over roots and rocks. When you are deep enough in your own nature to hear that everything can talk and may also be willing to listen, you say your piece. You make a full confession of whatever troubles you, what you blame yourself for, and what you blame on others. You let it all out. Maybe the beaver in the pond thwacks his tail to show he has heard you. Maybe a leaf blows into your hand. Maybe the world around you is unusually still, holding its breath. Whatever the response from nature, you have made what the Iroquois call the Confession on the Road. You will feel release and acceptance. And you may choose to receive the next things that you see or hear or feel as a response from the world that has heard you out.

In the Native American way, as Black Elk, the Lakota holy man, said, "The center of the world is wherever you are." For him, that was Harney Peak. For you, it is wherever you are living or traveling. You may find a special place in your everyday world. It may be just a corner of the garden, or a bench under a tree in the park, or that lake where you walk the dog. The more you go there, and open both your inner and outer senses, the more you will find that orenda has gathered there for you.

A woman who lives near the shore told me that she starts her day like this: "I go to the ocean in the morning at sunrise and put a hand in the water and say, 'Good morning, thank you, I love you.' I feel a response from this. The tide will suddenly surge up a little higher, hugging my feet, which is kind of cold in winter but wonderful in warmer weather. I talk to everything out loud like this."

This stirred my heart and set many chords of connection quivering. I thought of Jung's account of a conversation with Ochwiay Biano, an elder of the Taos Pueblo, during his visit to New Mexico. The elder complained that the "Americans" wanted to stamp out his religion and that this was evidence they were mad since "what we do, we do not only for ourselves but for the Americans also. We do it for the whole world."

Struggling to understand, Jung asked, "You think then, that

what you do in your religion benefits the whole world?" The elder replied, with great animation, "Of course. If we did not do it, what would become of the world?" He pointed to the sun and said, "We daily help our father to go across the sky."

The simple gesture of placing your hand in the sea, or on a tree, or on the earth, and expressing love and gratitude and recognition of the animate world around us is everyday church (as is dreamwork), good for us, and good for all our relations. "Things have a life of their own," as the gypsy says in *One Hundred Years of Solitude*. "It's simply a matter of waking up their souls."

It is good to do something every day, in any landscape, to affirm life in all that is around us. This may be especially important on days when the world seems drab and flat and even the eyes of other people in the street look like windows in which the blinds have been drawn down. The Longhouse People reminded me that the best kind of prayer is to give thanks to all our relations, to everything that supports life, and in doing so, to give our support to them. When I lived on a farm on the edge of Iroquois territory in upstate New York, I began each day by greeting the ancient oak on the dirt road behind the house as the elder of that land.

These days, it is often enough for me to say to sun and sky, whether on the sidewalk or in the park or by the sea:

I give thanks for the morning
I give thanks for the day
I give thanks for the gifts and the challenges of this
    lifetime

WYRD AND WEIRDER

Look north, just a short distance, from Jung's tower and his Trickster, and things get weird. Read the Eddas (literally the "great-grandmothers") and the Icelandic sagas with care, and you will find not only Viking battle stories, but some profound insights into the human condition and the interconnectedness of things.

The key word here is *Wyrd*, from which *weird* derives. *Wyrd* is Old English, of Germanic origin. It is often translated as "fate" or "destiny," but it is related to *weorthan*, which means "to become." Wyrd is best understood as a web of connection, joining everything that happens in this world to movements in other worlds.

Events that may appear to be separate in time or space are connected by threads that are fine, supple, and strong. Any movement in any part of the web may be felt anywhere else. Omens point to patterns; they are not just about something that is going to happen in the future. If you know the ways of Wyrd, you use them to read the patterns of connection. If you are a master of these things, you may be able to pull on the threads to change the patterns.

Wyrd is beyond the gods. The web precedes gods and men and lives after them. We call it a pattern, but like the Tao as it plays through the *Book of Changes*, Wyrd is in constant motion. A lively guide to these matters is Brian Bates' "documentary novel" *The Way of Wyrd*, where an Anglo-Saxon sorcerer instructs that "Wyrd itself is constant change, yet because it is created at every moment it is unchanging, like the still center of a whirlpool. All we can see are the ripples dancing on top of the water." Yes, by studying the ripples, you can detect what is moving at the bottom of the water or far away across its expanse.

Because we are part of Wyrd, we can never see the whole. So we look for ways to see enough to help us navigate. Carving and casting runes is a way. So are dreams and those special moments when you awaken to the workings of the deeper pattern. "Man is touched by wyrd when he becomes involved in matters whose nature and origins extend beyond existence on earth," Germanic scholar Paul Bauschatz explains. "There are times...when apparently ordinary activities acquire special significance, and it seems likely that at these times daily life is touched and colored with elements beyond our limited perceptions."

There is room to reweave the threads of Wyrd. Jenny Blain, who has participated in the revival of ancient Norse *seiðr*, or shamanic rituals, observes that "this concept of Wyrd is one that is being developed within the community. Though often translated as 'fate' and sometimes equated to 'karma,' it has a more dynamic sense. People are active agents in the creation of their own personal wyrd, or ørlög. Their deeds and vows, strands of ørlög, become part of the fabric of Wyrd." Those who work the seiðr rituals feel they are "'reading' Wyrd, seeing along the threads of the fabric to possible outcomes. Others within the community consider that seiðr in the past involved active interception of the fabric, 'tugging' at the threads."

In English, the word *weird* derives from *wyrd*. It declined from common usage in England until Shakespeare revived it, with a sinister twist, with the Weird Sisters in *Macbeth*. It retained some of its original meaning a little longer in Scotland, where if you called someone "weirdless," you were saying that he or she was unlucky.

In more recent times, to call something "weird" is to say that it is strange, uncanny, hard to explain, and maybe spooky. A "weirdo" is someone who is very strange. Yet thanks to a campaign that started in Austin, Texas, "weird" has been making a comeback. Austin is the first North American city to sprout a poster campaign to keep the city weird. *Keep Austin Weird*. Other cities followed suit.

One of my favorite books on Northern European traditions is *The Well of Remembrance* by Ralph Metzner, who embarked on a quest to reclaim the mythic wisdom of his ancestors from the Nazi curse. He was drawn to Odin, not as a war god, but as the poet-shaman wandering between the worlds, facilitating direct and personal revelation. In the course of his quest, he writes, "Often I felt as though I was seized, or inspired. I would think of Odin and get insights or answers to my questions, including questions about the meanings of certain myths. Or I would suddenly find pertinent myths that I had not known before. Strange though it may sound, I would have to say that much of what I am relating in this book has been directly given to me by Odin."

I have had similar experiences since Tolkien told me in a dream, many years ago, "You must study Scandinavian mythology." I was at first reluctant to follow that advice, partly because of the long shadow of the Nazi attempt to hijack the gods and symbols of the North. As I began to walk this ancestral path (I have Scandinavian blood on both sides of my family) in my reading and travel and in my dreams, I was rewarded by special moments of encounter and discovery that left me in no doubt that forces beyond the veil of the world were in play. During a trip to Europe, I had a personal vision of Yggdrasil, the World Tree, from which I wrote a poem.

The ancestors are calling, calling. And they can use the worldwide web as well as the web of the worlds. It is amusing to note that *wired* is an anagram for *weird*. A woman named Kim shared the following story:

SPIRIT LIKES THE WIRES

Spirit likes the wires. The web, in particular. The deities who work fate, don't they spin and snip threads? My mom's picture popped up on a dating app my ex-husband is on. He sent a screen shot. I'd just asked my mom that morning for a sign that she was there. He had been on that app over a year, and he showed me how faces appeared as you scrolled through and how you could indicate interest or not. My mom was never on a dating site, and certainly wouldn't be suitable to his selected age range. I think that via the web, we can have communication with the Other Side.

CLUSTER CHUCKS

The word *synchronicity* speaks only of things that happen at the same time, that are synchronous. But this is not the essence of the phenomenon. The experience of meaningful coincidence is not so much about things happening at the same time as it is about things happening in *a special moment* or a series of such moments. In such a moment, as Jung once said to Mircea Eliade, we may have the sense of a "rupture in time." When we observe a sequence or clustering of synchronistic events, we may sense that the rules of linear time have been suspended altogether. Things come together from across time or from outside time. Coincidence may run in a series, as *reincidence*, and we may feel its significance not only in one period of time, but in many. We may experience the phenomenon as a cluster of images and incidents, scattered over different places and times, that are connected by form and our sense of an underlying pattern.

Synchronicity, coincidence, correspondence, confluence, isomorphy, Tao, Speaking Land, Orenda, Wyrd — how can we best name, and account for, what is going on here?

My favorite explanation was provided by Einstein. He has appeared in a number of my dreams, talking in a stage German accent, sometimes at machine-gun speed, about such things as the physics of time travel and the code of the *I Ching*. Whoever my dream Einstein may be, behind the familiar mask, he has interesting things to reveal and to teach. Here is his demonstration of how synchronistic phenomena are generated, exactly as I recorded it in my dream journal on December 30, 2003:

EINSTEIN DEMONSTRATES PROBABILITY BUNDLES

A passage opens, like a long cylinder lined with silver and bronze-colored rods, angling up into the sky. As I speed up through it — shooting up effortlessly — I become aware that I am about to encounter someone who can instruct me on the workings of time and the content of the future. I come out high above the ground and look up at a huge revolving structure, something like a Ferris wheel on its side. At the end of each spoke is a different object, or rather bundle of objects. As the wheel revolves, I notice that the spokes go up and down at all angles, making the general shape of a sphere.

At the hub of the wheel is Einstein. He appears with his wild fluffy hair, in rumpled clothes, as he has appeared in other dreams. From the center, he works an engine that enables him to toss down bundles from the ends of the spokes. As one spoke dips, another rises, producing a seesaw effect. As the bundles fall to earth, Einstein instructs me that this is how the unfolding of events in time actually takes place: not in the serial fashion that is a concession to the limited human mind, but in the releasing of *probability bundles*, packages of time + energy whose contents will be unfolded over a certain period. The unfolding of events will be influenced by the dropping of subsequent probability bundles.

When I notice a riff of coincidence — things popping up that you *know* are connected, though there is no causation involved on the physical plane — I think of those probability bundles, fired from another world into this one, to burst across our space and time like multidimensional piñatas. The word *quantum* means "bundle" or "packet," so this image may be a clue to how quantum effects are manifested on a human scale.

What I like best about the dream image is that the machine

that fires the probability bundles closely resembles something you might find in an amusement park, evoking a game greater than the ones we spend most of our lives playing. Remember Heraclitus, who told us that the deepest logic of our lives is a child at play, moving pieces in a game, in another order of reality? Scholars cannot agree how to translate the word used for game pieces, *pesseuon*, in the fragment. Are the pieces in play something like dice? Dream Einstein has the solution: they are probability bundles.

Musing on this again, as I take the dog for his first walk along streets covered with snow and slush, I happen upon a discarded cider carton. In bold capitals, above a picture of a basket full of apples, is the text "CLUSTER CHUCKS." I smile at the echo of a certain off-color phrase. I nod in appreciation of the wit of whoever does the branding for the Woodchuck cider company. Then the excitement of the special moment grabs me. *Cluster chucks.* What a great name for what is going on when inner and outer events come together in one special moment, or a series of such moments, in ways that make sense even when they seem to defy reason.

CHAPTER THREE

BECOMING A KAIROMANCER

We are magnets in an iron globe. We have keys to all doors.
We are all inventors, each sailing out on a voyage of discovery,
guided each by a private chart, of which there is no duplicate.
The world is all gates, all opportunities,
strings of tension waiting to be struck.

— RALPH WALDO EMERSON, "RESOURCES"

Kairos is jump time, opportunity time, the special moment that you seize or miss. In Kairos moments, you may feel you have been released from linear time or that powers from outside time have irrupted into your world. The Greeks personified Kairos as a young, fleet-footed god, completely bald except for a curling lock falling over his forehead. Hence the phrase "seize time by the forelock." If you meet this fellow on the road and fail to seize the moment, you'll find him very hard to catch. Kairos is slippery.

Brutus talks about Kairos time, the time of opportunity, in a famous passage in Shakespeare's *Julius Caesar*:

There is a tide in the affairs of men,
Which, taken at the flood, leads on to fortune;

Omitted, all the voyage of their life
Is bound in shallows and in miseries.
On such a full sea are we now afloat,
And we must take the current when it serves
Or lose our ventures.

Kairos, in Greek, has related meanings in two interesting contexts: archery and weaving. In archery, *kairos* means an opening, in the specific sense of a long aperture through which the archer must make his arrow pass, as Odysseus, at the start of his battle with the suitors, must fire an arrow through the holes in a dozen ax heads standing in a row, in order to prove himself. Meeting the test of this kind of Kairos requires fine precision and the force to drive the arrow all the way through. In the art of weaving, *kairos* is the moment when the weaver must draw the yarn through the gap that opens — just for that moment — in the warp of the fabric that is being woven.

On the last day of a visit to the Bahamas, when I taught at the Sivananda Ashram on Paradise Island, I had an experience of Kairos that touched my heart. My programs were over. It was my last morning in the Bahamas, and I had packed my bags, ready to return to the frozen Northeast. I was due at the dock on the other side of the ashram in a couple of minutes, to catch the boat to Nassau en route to the airport. My hand was moving to shut down my laptop and tuck it away in my carry-on bag.

In this instant, I received a message from a dear friend and student. Could I possibly offer a seashell to the ocean for her deceased mother, who loved the ashram and stayed here many years ago?

There was no ticktock time to do this, but Kairos — and the heart — take precedence over Chronos. I ran down the steps to the white sand beach in front of the ashram and hunted up and down until I found a small white shell. I padded into the shallows and released the shell, gently, into the streaming hair of the sea goddess, with a prayer for my friend's mother. *May her paths be open.*

I caught my boat. When Kairos is in play, ordinary time is either suspended or elastic.

May we always be available to the Kairos moments when immediate action is required.

◆

Key elements in the experience of synchronicity that came into bold relief in the informal survey I reported in the last chapter include these: You know that coincidence is meaningful because *you feel it.* You know this is *a special moment*; sometimes it feels like time has stopped or, alternatively, as if something that is timeless has entered the realm of time. You may feel blessed or challenged by the presence of the numinous. And very often *you want to do something.* You want to say thank you; you want to tell other people; you want to check whether you have received a message and then figure out what to do about it.

In the ancient world, you knew a god was present because everything started to quiver or shimmer. The special moment was itself a god. We now know his name, Kairos. He is the antithesis of the old god Chronos. While Chronos represents linear time, the time that moves relentlessly in one direction, time that binds, Kairos represents that special moment in which you can break the bonds and operate in a spacious Now.

Thinking about the special quality of the Kairos moment, I want to offer a new word for the *practice* of navigating by synchronicity. The word is *kairomancy.* Translation: divination by special moments. Alternative version: making magic by seizing those special moments. Kairomancy trumps and contains other Mancies — bibliomancy, cartomancy, chiromancy, and their kin — as the Fool (to those who know the greater tarot) contains the secret of the whole deck and carries all the patterns of the world in his sack.

To become a kairomancer, you need to learn to trust your feelings as you walk the roads of this world, to develop your personal science of shivers, to recognize in your gut and your skin and in free-floating impressions that you know far more than you hold on the surface of consciousness. You need to take care of your poetic health, reading what rhymes in a day or a season. You want to expect the unexpected, to make friends with surprises, and never miss that special moment. The kairomancer understands that the time is always Now, except when the time is GO.

TWELVE RULES OF KAIROMANCY

1. WHATEVER YOU THINK OR FEEL, THE UNIVERSE SAYS YES

Whatever you think or feel, the universe says yes. Perhaps you have noticed this. Yes, we are talking about the law of attraction. It is indeed an ancient law, never a secret to those who live consciously. "All things which are similar and therefore connected, are drawn to each other's power," according to the medieval magus Heinrich Cornelius Agrippa von Nettesheim. It is a rule of reality that we attract or repel different things according to the emotions, the attitudes, the feelings, the agendas that we carry.

Before you walk into a room or turn a corner, your attitude is there already. It is engaged in creating the situation you are about to encounter. Whether you are remotely conscious of this or not, you are constantly setting yourself up for what the world is going to give you. If you go about your day filled with doom and gloom, the world will give you plenty of reasons to support that attitude. You'll start looking like that cartoon character who goes about with a personal black cloud over his head that rains only on his parade. Conversely, if your attitude is bright and open to happy surprises, you may be rewarded by a bright day, even when the sky is leaden overhead, and by surprisingly happy encounters.

Through energetic magnetism, we attract or repel people, events, and even physical circumstances according to the attitudes we embody. This process begins before we speak or act because thoughts and feelings are already actions and our attitudes are *out there* ahead of us. This requires us to do a regular attitude check, asking, *What attitude am I carrying? What am I projecting?*

It is not sufficient to do this on a head level. We want to check what we are carrying in our body and our energy field. If you go around carrying a repertoire of doom and gloom, you may not say what's on your mind, but the universe will hear you and support you. Attitude adjustment requires more than reciting the kind of New Age affirmation you see in cute boxes with flowers and sunsets on Facebook. It requires deeper self-examination and self-mobilization, and you can accomplish these in exercises you will find in chapter 4.

What are you doing? A woman in one of my workshops told me she hears this question, put by an inner voice, many times a day. Sometimes it rattles her and saps her confidence. But she is grateful for the inner questioner that provokes her to look at herself. It's a question worth putting to yourself any day. As you do that, remember that thinking and feeling are also *doing*.

"The passions of the soul work magic." I borrowed that from a medieval alchemist also beloved by Jung. It conveys something fundamental about our experience of how things manifest in the world around us. High emotions, high passions generate results. When raw energy is loose, it has effects in the world. It can blow things up or bring them together. There is an art in learning to operate when your passions are riding high and to recognize that is a moment when you can make magic. Even when you are in the throes of what people would call negative emotions — rage, anger, pain, grief, even fear — if you can take the force of such emotions and choose to harness and direct them in a certain creative or healing way, you can work wonders, and you can change the world around you.

How? Because there is no impermeable barrier between mind and matter. Jung and Pauli in concert, the great psychologist and the great physicist, came around to the idea that the old medieval phrase applies: *unus mundus*, "one world." *Psyche* and *physis*, mind and matter, are one reality. They interweave at every level of the universe. They are not separate. As Pauli wrote, "Mind and body could be interpreted as complementary aspects of the same reality." I think this is fundamental truth, and it becomes part of fundamental life operation when you wake up to it.

The stronger our emotions, the stronger their effects on our psychic and physical environment. And the effects of our emotions may reach much further than we can initially understand. They can generate a convergence of incidents and energies, for good or bad, in ways that change *everything* in our lives and can affect the lives of many others.

When we think or feel strongly about another person, we *will* touch that person and affect his or her mind and body — even across great distances — unless that person has found a way to block that transmission. The great French novelist Honoré de Balzac wrote that "ideas are projected as a direct result of the force by which they are conceived and they strike wherever the brain sends them by a mathematical law comparable to that which directs the firing of shells from their mortars."

Bring in the creative imagination, and it is wonderful how the world can rearrange itself. I heard a beautiful little story about this from a friend in California. She had been consciously building a kind of inner sanctuary, a place of peace and joy where she could take herself anytime in her imagination. She envisioned a lovely place with healing waters, around an oak tree she knows in the natural world. In imagination, she added a swing to the tree, visualizing the ropes fastened to one of its great limbs. She pictured herself rocking happily under the spreading canopy of the oak. She used this image to help her get through a long and sleepless night when she was severely ill.

A week later, feeling much restored, she took a hike to the place of the oak. And found that someone had added a swing, exactly where she had placed it in her imagination.

Scientific experiments have shown the ability of the human mind and emotions to change physical matter: studies by Masaru Emoto have shown that human emotions can change the nature and composition of water, and the Findhorn experiments have taught us that good thoughts positively affect the growth of plants. Conversely, rage or grief can produce disturbing and sometimes terrifying effects in the physical environment.

"We are magnets in an iron globe," declared Emerson. If we are upbeat and positive, "we have keys to all doors.... The world is all gates, all opportunities, strings of tension waiting to be struck." Conversely, "A low, hopeless spirit puts out the eyes; skepticism is slow suicide. A philosophy which sees only the worst ... dispirits us; the sky shuts down before us."

Kairomancers know that whatever our circumstances, we always have the power to choose our attitude, and that this can change everything.

2. CHANCE FAVORS
THE PREPARED MIND

Remember CLUSTER CHUCKS, the name on the abandoned cider carton I found on the sidewalk while thinking about ways to describe synchronicity and probability bundles? The cider carton with the naughty name is an example of a sidewalk oracle. Such oracles often speak most eloquently when we are not looking for anything in particular but have something on our mind or in our heart to which the world may provide an answer or a commentary. In such encounters, we will notice the truth of Pasteur's observation that "chance favors the prepared mind." Someone else, confronted by the CLUSTER CHUCKS carton, might have muttered something about college kids trashing the neighborhood or merely chuckled over the play on another phrase. For me, the name on the box was both a confirmation of a line of thought and the gift of a fun, colloquial way to name a phenomenon that often eludes tagging.

In *The Three "Only" Things*, I reviewed the extraordinary role of chance, in the form of laboratory "accidents" and "accidental" discoveries, in the history of science and invention. Alfred Nobel produced gelignite — a more stable explosive than dynamite, which he also invented — when he accidentally mixed collodion (guncotton) with nitroglycerin. Swiss chemist Albert Hofmann discovered the properties of LSD by accidentally ingesting it at his lab.

Alexander Fleming discovered penicillin because he neglected to isolate bacterial cultures from stray spores blowing around in his hospital building — notably from a mycologist's lab on the floor below. Fleming went away on vacation. When he returned, he found that penicillin mold had killed his bacteria — and saw with his trained eye an extraordinary cure.

Rayon was discovered by the French chemist Hilaire de

Chardonnet, an assistant to Louis Pasteur, when he spilled a bottle of collodion and later noticed that as the liquid evaporated, it changed into a viscous substance from which thin fibers could be drawn.

The secret of America's favorite breakfast cereal was discovered when the Kellogg brothers left cooked wheat untended for a day and then found that when they tried to roll the mass, they got flakes instead of a sheet. Charles Goodyear learned how to vulcanize rubber — producing the automobile tire and spawning the automotive revolution in transportation — after he accidentally left a mixture on a hot plate that turned into hard rubber.

Smart luck, rather than dumb luck, is involved in such inventions and discoveries. The beneficiaries of chance were prepared to take advantage of the Kairos moments they were given because they knew the fields of possibility that were being opened. They had done the work that made them ready for the divine play. Anyone unprepared would have dismissed the accidents and kitchen errors as irritations or unpleasant messes instead of unexpected solutions, vital clues, or course correction.

Kairomancers *attract* the right kind of accidents. In a study of creative genius, John Briggs observed that "creators actively court chance. They're always ready to notice and amplify with insight some accident of their environment virtually everybody else thinks is trivial or fails to notice. This capacity is, in a deep sense, what makes creators creative." Creative writers know this well. As Roberto Calasso observes, "The writing of a book gets under way when the writer discovers that he is magnetized in a certain direction.... Then everything he comes across — even a poster or a sign or a newspaper headline or words heard by chance in a café or in a dream — is deposited in a protected area like material waiting to be elaborated."

3. YOUR OWN WILL COME TO YOU

Your own will come to you. AE (the visionary writer and artist George Russell) summarized the law of spiritual gravitation in this phrase. It is a vital truth. AE also wrote: "I found that every intense imagination, every new adventure of the intellect [is] endowed with magnetic power to attract to it its own kin. Will and desire were as the enchanter's wand of fable, and they drew to themselves their own affinities.... One person after another emerged out of the mass, betraying their close affinity to my moods as they were engendered."

If the passions of our souls are strong enough, they may draw "lifelong comrades." In his beautiful little book *The Candle of Vision*, AE gave a personal example. When he first attempted to write verse, he immediately met a new friend, a dreaming boy "whose voice was soon to be the most beautiful voice in Irish literature." This was of course William Butler Yeats. "The concurrence of our personalities seemed mysterious and controlled by some law of spiritual gravitation."

In his later life, AE found a soul companion in the Australian writer P. L. Travers, the author of *Mary Poppins* and also a deep student of the Western Mysteries and a world-class mythographer. AE wrote to P. L. Travers about a further aspect of spiritual gravitation: "I feel I belong to a spiritual clan whose members are scattered all over the world and these are my kinsmen." The principle that your own will come to you is especially important in forging life relationships. In preparing this book, I asked several hundred people who follow my work to report on special moments and synchronicity that opened or deepened their connections with special people — lovers and partners, mentors and soul friends. In the context of love and marriage, the title of Toye Elizabeth's tale of everyday magic is quite entertaining:

RETAKING THE BIOLOGY CLASS

It was spring quarter in college, and I had decided at the last minute to retake a biology class that I slept through as a freshman, in hopes of getting a better grade. I had started having dreams and strong attraction to tall guys with wavy auburn hair, out of the blue. These traits had never been on my radar before. I pushed the fantasies aside, telling myself I was going to concentrate on school only that quarter.

The class was strangely empty. I got that sense of déjà vu. Everything was odd and yet familiar. I knew somebody here. I turned around to look and saw the tall guy with auburn hair from my dreams. In the same instant, he turned to look at me.

We started talking after that, and as soon as I looked into his big brown eyes, time stopped. I felt at home when I was with him. Everything about this felt right and safe, yet also charged with magic. We'd be talking and the music playing in a space would give us the same words we were thinking or saying to each other. We would go our separate ways and meet each other at the same places in ways we did not plan.

A year later, at our wedding, the best man said in his speech that our first day in class was not a real class day at all, which is why the lab was so empty. He also said that when my husband went back to the apartment they shared at the time, he said he had just met the girl he was going to marry. He then started going in to class early to get a seat at the front. He would put his books on the seat next to him to save it for me and make sure we would sit together. Thirty years into our marriage, he tells me that he has loved me before we met in this lifetime. We are still generating synchronicity — songs that speak our unspoken thoughts, him calling me just as I pick up the phone to call him.

It is an old and true saying that when the student is ready, the teacher will appear. Deborah gives a moving personal account of how that has worked for her:

OUT OF THE BOX

I have met my teachers through synchronicity. My husband died suddenly, tragically, in Horta on our boat where we lived. I came home to Maine and took a job selling yachts. Part of the job included using the Excel program.

One day I looked at the screen and realized I was spending my days putting numbers in square boxes. So I quit.

The day I left my job, I walked down Main Street. I paused in front of the museum to watch a Tibetan monk. He was in the window, constructing a mandala. I watched, spellbound by the care with which he was making the circles, grain by grain. He became my teacher. It was a very special moment. I rejected a life in a box and immediately met a teacher who creates circles to be blown away. I have been friends with that monk for fifteen years.

What we feed our minds and our bodies attracts or repels different parts of ourselves as well as different people and different classes of spirits.

I have noticed in my own life as a writer that when I am seeking to create something new, and taking risks is involved, I draw the interest of greater powers. More of my own creative spirit becomes engaged, lending me abilities beyond those I possess when I am doing something small and safe. I notice this as a teacher and healer. When I am willing to give more to others, to do my very best to bring the light or spirit into their eyes or to wrap them in the healing embrace of Great Mother Bear, I draw powers far beyond my ordinary self — and now it can be very important to let the ordinary self stand aside while a Greater Self operates.

4. YOU LIVE IN THE SPEAKING LAND

We live in a conscious universe, where everything is alive, everything is connected, everything has spirit. Early peoples say that humans are the animals that tell stories about all the others, but this does not mean that humans are the only ones talking. Birds speak in complex languages; bees are great communicators, and their drone or hum is the sound that humans often hear when their inner senses are opening. A stone can speak, though it may lie dormant and silent until approached in the right way. A river or a mountain can speak. Thunder was louder than any human could speak until people started making things that can blow up cities.

As Australian Aborigines say, we live in a Speaking Land. How well we can hear depends on how we use our senses, both inner and outer. How much we can use and understand depends on selection, on grasping what matters.

One summer, en route to a lake in the woods where I like to swim, I stopped at a friend's house. She appeared at the side of the house, pressing a finger to her lips while beckoning to me with the other hand. When I walked quietly over to her, I saw, ten feet away around the corner of the house, a young black bear. He stared at me intently for what seemed like a long time before ambling away into the woods. As he moved, I noticed he was hobbling; one of his legs was injured.

I have felt a very strong connection with the Bear for more than twenty-five years, ever since I met the Bear in a series of life-changing dreams and learned that, in North America, the medicine bear is a tremendous power for healing and protection. So I was deeply impressed with the unexpected meeting with the black bear on the grass, and was concerned about the condition of its leg.

I did not realize that there was a quite specific message for me in this sighting until, one week later, I fell and injured my leg, severing one of the muscles that compose the quadriceps. Now I, too, was hobbling with an injured leg. Six weeks later, just before I went in for a consultation with an orthopedist to determine whether I should undergo knee surgery, my friend called me to say she had seen the black bear again and his leg was fine. This gave me high hopes for my own leg. The orthopedist was amazed by the strength and mobility I had regained in my leg and told me, "You are either very odd or very lucky," and that no surgery would be required — just more swimming and walking in the woods.

Spirits of place include the spirits and holographic memories of humans who have lived and loved and struggled on the land before us. I once led a favorite workshop on "Making Death Your Ally" at a retreat site near the Gettysburg battlefield. It was not really a surprise when I noticed, through my inner senses, that we had been joined by the spirits of several hundred men in blue and gray, soldiers killed on both sides in the American Civil War who had apparently remained close to the place where their bodies had fallen. I requested their senior officers to step forward. I suggested to them that they were welcome to audit our class but that it was primarily intended for the living who had joined our circle and that I would be grateful if they would remain outside our perimeter and maintain good order. I have rarely felt that one of my workshop groups has received so much psychic protection! I give specific practical guidance on discerning and dealing with spirits of the deceased in my books *Dreamgates* and *The Dreamer's Book of the Dead*.

5. GROW YOUR POETIC HEALTH

"The bottom of the mind is paved with crossroads," wrote the French poet Paul Valéry. This marvelous, mysterious line stirs up the imagination. It encourages us to think about how on the surface of the mind we may have been shortchanging ourselves. We may have been snagging ourselves in limited, linear thinking, even trapping ourselves in mental boxes.

Life is full of crossroads. We often rush through them without noticing the choices that were open in a Kairos moment. Or else we see our choices in false absolutes, duty versus pleasure, good versus bad, black or white. In the deeper mind, we are ready to take a more spacious view and roam with more freedom in the garden of forking paths, even to see that Yogi Berra may have spoken truth when he said, "If you come to a fork in the road, take it."

Kairomancers take care of their poetic health by developing a tolerance for ambiguity and a readiness to see more angles and options than the surface mind perceives. They grow poetic health by cultivating that "talent for resemblances" that two wise Greeks, Aristotle and Artemidorus, both held to be the primary qualification for a dream interpreter — and that is no less a vital prerequisite for recognizing signs and symbols in waking life.

Mark Twain is supposed to have said that history rhymes. I don't know whether he really said that or not. The words have not been found in the canonical texts of this wonderfully noncanonical humorist. I do know that life rhymes. We notice recurring themes and symbols in dreams: running late for the plane, not prepared for the test, trying to keep the bear out of the living room. In the same way, we notice that themes and situations recur in everyday life.

Pay attention when the same theme, or symbol, or image comes up again and again, just as you might pay attention to recurring dreams. When a theme or situation comes at you again and again in dreams, that is often a signal that there is a message coming through that you need to read correctly — and that, beyond merely getting the message, you need to do something about it, to take action. It is the same with rhyming sequences and repeating symbols in waking life.

When you begin to notice a repetition of a certain situation in life, you may say, "Okay, we're going around the track again. Maybe I want to make sure that I'm not just going around and around in my life in circles of repetition, but that I am on a spiral path." Which would mean that each time life loops around to where you think you were before, you've risen to a slightly higher level, so you can see things with greater awareness and, hopefully, make better choices.

There is a whole education in the art of poetic living in Baudelaire's poem "Correspondances":

La Nature est un temple où de vivants piliers
Laissent parfois sortir de confuses paroles;
L'homme y passe à travers des forêts de symboles
Qui l'observent avec des regards familiers.

Nature is a temple whose living pillars
Sometimes let slip mysterious messages;
We walk here through a forest of symbols
That watch us with knowing eyes.

[My free translation]

Baudelaire, the urban dandy, has it exactly right: we are walking in a forest of living symbols that are looking at us. When we are in a state of poetic health, we understand that "the imagination is the most scientific of the faculties, because it is the only one to understand the universal analogy, or that which a mystical religion calls correspondence."

Les parfums, les couleurs et les sons se répondent.

Perfumes, colors, and sounds correspond.
[Baudelaire, "Correspondances," my free translation]

In the midst of leading a workshop titled "Dreaming Like an Egyptian" in Ann Arbor, I stopped for breakfast at a Whole Foods store. As I munched my mini-baguette — my favorite breakfast — I talked to my coordinator and a couple of wonderful dreamers who were attending the workshop about the significance of snakes in the Egyptian maps of the Otherworld. Snakes appear all over — as adversaries, as protectors, or simply as guardians whose function is to make us brave up and prove we are ready to progress to the really good stuff.

When Ra journeys in his solar boat, accompanied by Creative Utterance (Hu), Insight (Sia), and Magic (Heka), he is shielded and enclosed by the Mehen serpent, whose name means "the Enveloper." He is opposed by the cosmic adversary, Apophis, also depicted as a serpent, of the world-devouring kind.

The Egyptians symbolized awakened psychospiritual power with the *wadjet*, or uraeus serpent, the cobra that features on the crowns of pharaohs. The raised head evokes the opened third eye of vision and the ability to operate from this center.

Wadjet is also a snake goddess, patron of Lower Egypt, protector of kings and of Horus, closely allied — in evolving mythology — with both the cat goddess Bast and the vulture goddess Nekhbet. Her name means "papyrus colored."

We spoke of our own associations with snakes and the many different ways snakes can figure in dreams. We talked of the snake's power to shed its skin and of the importance of the serpent as a symbol — for the vital energy of life, the kundalini force, and in medicine and healing.

After half an hour of this lively, serpentine conversation, it was time to move on to start day two of the workshop. I reflected on how, in our opening session, we had called the serpent energy up through the soles of the feet, and through the energy centers of the body, to open the third eye. I had invited our adventurers to do the full Egyptian by picturing the *wadjet* cobra at the vision center, and then rising from there to fly above the landscape like a bird.

In the parking lot, right in front of us, we discovered a sleek, powerful convertible painted Egyptian blue. On the front was a silver cobra. On a side panel was a larger cobra that seemed to quiver, ready to strike, against the mirror-bright surface of the car. I walked around the back and found the cobra again, in a crest, and the make of the car. I was looking at a Shelby GT 500. I looked it up and found that it is a high-performance version of the Ford Mustang, retail price around fifty-five thousand dollars, advertising slogan: "Coiled and ready to strike."

Life rhymes, and it hisses.

6. COINCIDENCE MULTIPLIES ON THE ROAD

This refers both to outer movement and to inner transitions, especially when either carries you outside your normal rounds. You're not just going through the constant rounds of your life. You're out and about. You're going somewhere new.

Maybe you're crossing a border. Maybe you're getting on and off planes or trains. You're out and about. In movement in the world, you tend to drop your normal, routine pattern of perceptions and notice some different things because you're in a different landscape.

Nonetheless, unless you've changed your eyes, you won't see the new things. You have to have different eyes in order to see different landscapes. Even so, it is generally true that when we are in movement, not in the familiar rut, we are more likely to notice and to generate and experience coincidence.

The bigger side of it is that when we are in motion in terms of life passages, including challenging passages, when we are falling in or out of love, falling in or out of relationships, when birth or death is in the field, coincidence tends to multiply not just in our perception, but in objective reality. It multiplies because everything is astir. Things are not constant. They are themselves in motion.

The Vapor Drinker and the Hungry Road

I took the road with me on a trip to Santa Fe for a board meeting of the Society of Shamanic Practitioners. My in-flight novel was *The Famished Road*, an extraordinary novel by Nigerian author Ben Okri. I was seized by the first lines, which I read over and over, to let the mystery move through me while I tried to fathom it: "In the beginning there was a river. The river became a road and the road branched out to the whole world. And because the road was once a river it was always hungry."

The narrator is a boy of the kind called *abiku* in Nigeria, who may be fated to die young because he has spirit companions on the Other Side who want him to return to them soon and will do almost anything to pull him out of the land of the living. Madame Koto's palm-wine bar is his constant hangout, and its clientele makes the denizens of the space bar in *Star Wars* look like country club golfers in plaid pants.

I was seized by descriptions of how, as the living raise a glass or a fork or a cigarette to their lips, the spirits pressing thick about them dive in to get the first taste. The spirits drink the vapor of booze or food or smokes rather than the solid stuff. By my experience and observation, this is very much how it is, though few in modern Western society are able to perceive it. I have never met a genuine alcoholic, for example, who is not afflicted by a press of dead drunks trying to get another drink — that is to say, the spirit of the bottle — through them.

I was thinking about this when I deplaned at Albuquerque airport. On my way down to baggage claim, I was greeted by a crescent line of cheery people ringing handbells, with a large explanatory sign that read: "ENCHANTMENT. Albuquerque Handbells Ensemble." Nice.

As I rode the last escalator down, I was astonished to see a lean man in dark glasses puffing on a cigarette. Not something you expect to see in a U.S. airport these days. When I got closer, I saw that he was not blowing smoke. Rather, as he sucked on the tube, a fine mist — a vapor — rose around him.

After I took my seat at the front of the airport shuttle, he came up the steps, still sucking on the strange cigarette. "Excuse me," I spoke to him. "I would like to know about your ghost cigarette."

He took this as an invitation to take the vacant seat next to me. He explained how the e-cigarette, as he called it, simulates the act of tobacco smoking by using heat to vaporize a propylene glycol liquid solution into an aerosol mist that is inhaled.

I told him about the vapor drinkers in the novel. "When I saw you, I thought a character had stepped out of Madame Koto's bar." He laughed and shared part of his life story. A writer and artist, he has traveled the two worlds, experimenting with lucid dreaming and the shamanic use of hallucinogens. He quickly agreed with me that the most powerful dreamers and shamans have no need of chemicals beyond those produced in their own bodies. He told me about his friend Francis Huxley's early work in Amazonia and Haiti, adding two books to my always immense reading list.

He had lived in Bali and gave me a thrilling, step-by-step account of rituals of village exorcism in which the powers of good must be mustered against evil spirits led by the terrifying demon queen, Rangda. All of this made for a wonderfully fast and fun ride from Albuquerque to Santa Fe.

Manhattan Transfer

An airport lounge is the model of a liminal space, and I stop at many. I got up at midnight to work on this book before rushing to the airport to catch a predawn flight, then stopped in at a bar at O'Hare while waiting for my second flight of the day. It was only 10:00 AM, but I had earned a beer. I was joined at the bar by a well-dressed older woman who asked the bartender for a manhattan. That's a classy bourbon cocktail you don't often hear ordered in midmorning, except maybe by Don Draper in *Mad Men*.

Before the bartender had mixed the drink, she switched her order to bourbon with ginger ale. I could not resist. I said to this stranger, "You raised the tone of this establishment and then you dropped it down again."

She laughed, then peered at me and screeched, "We know each other!" I did not recognize her until she reminded me that she had attended some of my workshops twenty years before and had joined a group I led on an adventure in the high Andes. We had not seen each other since. How come she was in the bar now? She explained that three of her flights had been canceled and she had to stay overnight at an airport hotel.

"Do you have a story for me?" I asked.

"I've been going deeper into Buddhism," she replied. "I just came from a Buddhist retreat in Wisconsin."

"Okay. Always good to ground and balance after something like that. Cheers!" We clinked glasses. I am an Australian. I'll have a beer anytime I feel like it when traveling, but I'll leave the morning manhattan to someone coming off a Buddhist retreat.

She wanted to talk about karma.

I told her that I think there are consequences for everything we do and that it is important to consider how we are collecting karma of every kind in our present lives, as well as carrying karma from other lives. "I like the Buddhist idea that we can be released from all of that in the moment of enlightenment. Tathagata time!" We toasted again.

More serious now, I reflected on the apparent contradiction between the idea of linear karma and the probability that in the multidimensional universe, everything is going on Now — and on limitless parallel event tracks.

"If I think that my life is linked to the dramas of other people in other times and that I have inherited karma from what they did or did not do, maybe I can reach back to them, launching from the moment of Now. Maybe my thoughts and actions now help or hinder in their own time — which is also now — and may be more helpful as I rise to greater consciousness of how all this works."

It is possible to operate with these two seemingly contradictory visions of reality: linear karma in Chronos time and the simultaneity of experience in the multiverse in a spacious Now. It is like the observation in physics that something can be both a particle and a wave, and you will see it one way or the other according to how you observe it.

7. BY WHAT YOU FALL, YOU MAY RISE

For every setback, look for opportunity. That is a provocative statement, hard to accept when you feel betrayed or shamed or in the depths of grief or loss. When you have lost your job, or your partner has walked out on you, or you have made the worst mistake of your life, how can you accept the idea that "by what you fall, you can rise"?

You have nothing to lose by proceeding *as if*, despite appearances, there may be a gift in the loss. You can try saying to yourself, *Okay. That went down the tube. That door closed. Wait a minute. If that door closed, where's the door that might be opening?*

You may want to consider the cases of people who have been savagely beaten down by life only to rise again, showing us that there can be a tremendous gift in a wound. I think of Harriet Tubman, the most famous conductor of the Underground Railroad, who helped hundreds of fugitive slaves escape to freedom in the North in the years before the American Civil War. Aged about eleven, she was nearly killed when she was hit in the forehead by a two-pound lead weight hurled by an angry overseer. She carried the scar for the rest of her life. One of the effects of the wound was that she developed a form of narcolepsy that required her to take short and sudden "sleeps" in the middle of any kind of activity. It was during those sleeps that she saw visions that showed her the roads and river fords and safe houses to which she was able to guide escaping slaves, avoiding the slave owners' posses.

When we are seized by terrible emotions of rage or grief in our own lives, we can choose to try to harness the raw energy involved and turn it — like a fire hose — toward creative or healing action.

You will want to remember that on a path of transformation, you reach a point where you break down or you break through, and sometimes the breakdown comes before the breakthrough.

Sometimes a fair amount of Chronos time is required to appreciate what Emerson called "the compensations of calamity." He wrote that such compensations become apparent "after long intervals of time. A fever, a mutilation, a cruel disappointment, a loss of wealth, a loss of friends, seems at the moment unpaid loss, and unpayable. But the sure years reveal the remedial force that underlies all facts."

8. INVOKED OR UNINVOKED, GODS ARE PRESENT

"I was just walking Zeus," the dog walker greets me on the sidewalk. "He's in a very good mood today."

This is excellent news, even (or especially) if the Zeus in question is a large black Lab mix. God is dog spelled backward. Anyone who knows anything about gods knows that they don't stay in one form.

The mug on my desk has the motto *Vocatus atque non vocatus deus aderit* (Invoked or uninvoked, the god is present). This is the inscription Jung carved over the entrance to his home on the lake. The mug holds pens and pencils I reach for every day.

"Coincidence is God's way of remaining anonymous," goes that old saying. This is certainly the view of ancient and indigenous peoples, though they would prefer to say "gods" rather than "God." The Stoics maintained that divination is possible because there are gods and they wish to communicate with humans. "If there is divination, there are gods; if there are gods, there is divination," as Cicero summarized the argument in his treatise *De divinatione*.

Living in the vicinity of Zurich, city of bankers and cuckoo clocks, and mentored by Freud, who was a self-declared atheist and skeptic, Jung invented a language of "archetypes" for public use, in place of the old talk of gods and spirits. But the old gods continued to dominate his imagination, and they even exerted a hold on Freud, who surrounded himself with an army of statuettes of deities from all over the ancient world and refused to travel without at least a platoon of these "old and grubby gods."

When Jung speaks of archetypes as dynamic forces emerging from the collective unconscious and working effects in the mind and in the world, he is talking about powers that most human cultures have recognized as gods or spirits. In his essay "The Spirit of

Psychology," Jung describes an encounter with the archetypes as an experience of the "holy." He observes that it can be both healing and destructive and that no one who has gone through this experience remains unchanged. The archetypes are not subject to time and space.

Canadian dream teacher Nance Thacker recalls: "When I was a kid, I used to think the gods, goddesses, and our ancestors were playing with us, setting up the scenarios and making bets as to what we'd do. Sometimes they'd slip us a little hint about something that was to come or give us a little nudge to remind us that they were there in the form of synchronicities, déjà vu, and the like (though I didn't have words for the experience at the time)."

Perhaps we need to return to the wisdom of the child and the ancients. While the world around us is alive and spirited, it is also the playground or boxing ring for spirits whose home is in other realities. Some have been worshipped as gods, invoked as angels, or feared as demons, and still are by many. A passage in the Puranas informs us that there are forty thousand orders of beings, humanoid to human perception, that are within contact range of humans. They may be friendly, hostile, or inimical to humans and human agendas.

For the ancients, the manifestation of a god did not necessarily remove the need to do some fact-checking or at least get a second opinion. There is a most illuminating story about this in the *Odyssey*. The hero, Odysseus, has survived sea monsters and sirens and the wrath of a sea god and is at last on his home island. But he has been away for ten years since going off to war, and almost everyone believes he is dead. His palace is full of brutish and lustful men, suitors vying for the hand of his wife, Penelope, and with it, his kingdom. Their appetites are laying waste to his livestock, his wine cellar, and his female servants.

At the prompting of his constant guide, who is no less than

the goddess Athena, Odysseus has disguised himself in the rags of a beggar, with a funny traveler's hat. He is mocked and scorned by the suitors and even some of his own retainers. Nobody recognizes him. They will find it hard to recognize him even when he shows himself in a different form. His homeland seems stranger to him than the magic realms from which he has returned. He must be asking himself, *Which is the dream?* He may be wondering whether he is dead.

He spends a sleepless night, tossing and turning. The "man of many ways" is seeking a way to expel the suitors who have taken over his home. But they are many, and he is one; and even if he finds a way to kill them all, their kinsmen will come to take revenge. The goddess Athena now appears to him in mortal form, "swooping down from the sky in a woman's build and hovering at his head." She wants to know why he is still awake, fretting and exhausting himself. Why does he distrust her when she assures him that he will gain victory that day? Athena promises that he will gain victory "even if fifty bands of mortal fighters closed around us, hot to kill us off in battle" — because she is with him.

Athena "showered sleep across his eyes," but when Odysseus wakes, on the morning of Apollo's feast day, even the promise of a goddess is not enough. He wants further signs. He speaks to the All-Father, Zeus. "Show me a sign." In fact, Odysseus asks for two signs, "a good omen voiced by someone awake, indoors" and "another sign, outside, from Zeus himself."

He is answered at once by a great roll of thunder, out of a clear blue sky.

Then he hears a "lucky word" from a woman grinding grain inside the halls. Hearing thunder from a cloudless sky, the woman recognizes a sign from Zeus.

She speaks aloud to the king of the gods:

Sure it's a sign you're showing someone now.
So, poor as I am, grant my prayer as well;
let this day be the last, the last these suitors
bolt their groaning feasts in King Odysseus' house!

The twin oracles — from the sky and from overheard speech
— harden Odysseus' resolve, and the scene is set for the astonishing slaughter of the suitors under the rain of arrows from the bow that none but the hero (and his son) can bend. In Robert Fagles' translation, book 20 of the *Odyssey* is given the title "Portents Gather," and it is a good one. Here we see oracles speak in ways the Greeks observed closely and valued highly: through brontomancy (divination by thunder) and by listening for kledons (overheard speech or sound).

In the *Odyssey*, as in ancient Greek society, dreams and visions are the most important mode of divination. Yet our understanding of dreams may be deceptive, as Penelope explains in book 19 when she speaks of the since-famous gates of ivory and horn. So even when blessed by a direct encounter with a goddess, the hero turns to the world around him for confirmation.

Consciously or unconsciously, we walk on a kind of mythic edge. Just behind that gauzy veil of ordinary understanding, there are other powers, beings who live in the fifth dimension or dimensions beyond. To them, our lives may be as open as the lives of others would be to us if we could fly over the rooftops — and nobody had a roof on their house, and we could look in and see it from every possible angle.

A kairomancer is always going to be willing to *look for the hidden hand* in the play of coincidence, and to turn to more than one kind of oracle to check on the exact nature of the game.

9. YOU WALK IN MANY WORLDS

Part of the secret logic of our lives may be that our paths constantly interweave with those of numberless parallel selves, sometimes converging or even merging, sometimes diverging ever farther. The gifts and failings of these alternate selves — with all the baggage train of their separate lives — may influence us, when our paths converge, in ways that we generally fail to recognize. Yet a sudden afflux of insight or forward-moving energy may be connected with joining up with an alternate and lively self, just as a sour mood of defeat or a series of otherwise inexplicable setbacks may relate to the shadow of a different parallel self, a Sad One or a Dark One.

It is possible that every choice we make spins off a parallel event track with different outcomes. This is becoming the mainstream view of physics, as in Many Worlds theory. In this multidimensional universe, in our multidimensional self, we are connected to many counterpart personalities living in other times, other probable realities, other dimensions. According to the choices that we make and the dramas that we live, we sometimes come closer to them; and sometimes, in a sense, we step through a portal, we step through an opening between the worlds, we step through an interdimensional membrane, and our issues and our lives and our dramas and our gifts and our karma are joined.

Then there is our relationship to other personalities, living in the past or future, whose dramas are connected to our own and may all be going on simultaneously. I think of a Mongolian warrior shaman who appeared in a recent dream, standing at a threshold. Behind him is a vast plain — a plain of battle, a plain of struggle. He is wearing a long, heavy coat of skins and furs. His headdress is a helmet with furs. He has bronze shaman's mirrors and metal charms all over him. I look at this man in my dream, standing in the threshold between his reality and mine. I know that he is living at least eight centuries ago, yet we are connected now. We know each other. We are connected in a multidimensional drama, and this may generate events in both our lives that will appear as "chance" to those who cannot find the transtemporal pattern.

Such connections may be triggered by travel. You go to a new place, and you encounter the spirits of that land — including personalities that may be part of your own multidimensional story.

Jane Roberts' account of how this works, in the *Seth* books that she channeled and in her own *Oversoul Seven* novels, is the clearest and most coherent that I have so far discovered.

Part of the secret logic of our lives is that we are all connected to *counterpart personalities* — Seth calls them "probable selves" — living in other times and other probable universes. Their gifts and challenges can become part of our current stories, not only through linear karma, but through the interaction now across time and dimensions. The dramas of past, future, or parallel personalities can affect us now. We can help or hinder each other.

In the model of understanding I have developed, this family of counterpart souls is joined on a higher level by a sort of hub personality, an "oversoul," a higher self within a hierarchy of higher selves going up and up. The choices that you make, the moves that you make, can attract or repel other parts of your larger self.

The hidden hand suggested by synchronistic events may be that of another personality within our multidimensional family, reaching to us from what we normally perceive as past or future, or from a parallel or other dimension.

10. MARRY YOUR FIELD

"The poet marries the language, and out of this marriage the poem is born." This beautiful, passionate statement was made by

W. H. Auden, and it takes us right inside the crucible in which all creative action is born. It's sexy, it's spiritual, it makes your heart beat faster, it puts a champagne fizz of excitement into the air. It suffuses everything around with incredible light, so you feel you are seeing the curve of a flower stem or the bubbles in a glass for the very first time.

Such depth, such passion, such focused rapture is not only the province of poets, though we may need poetic speech to suggest what and how it is. Are you with me now? I am talking about you, and me, and the creative leap we can and will make as the year turns. The essence of the creative act is to bring something new into the world. You may have no earthly idea, at this moment, about how exactly you can do that.

So let me offer some eminently practical guidance, based on what Auden said about the roots of creation: start by marrying your field.

What is your field? It's not work in the ordinary sense, or what your diplomas say you are certified to do, or how you describe yourself in a job résumé — although it can encompass all of those things. Your field is where you ache to be. Your field is what you will do, day or night, for the sheer joy of the doing, without counting the cost or the consequences. Your field is the territory within which you can do the Work that your deeper life is calling you to do. Your field is not limitless. You can't bring anything into creative manifestation without accepting a certain form or channel, which requires you to set limits and boundaries. So your field is also the place within which the creative force that is in you will develop a form.

If you are going to bring something new into your world, find the field you will marry, as the poet marries language, as the artist marries color and texture, as the chef marries taste and aroma, as the swimmer marries the water.

Let's say that you have a notion that your creative act may

involve writing. Maybe you even think you have a book, or a story or screenplay, in you. For you, marrying the field will require you to marry words and be their constant lover. You'll engage in orgies of reading, have tantric sex with a first (or third) draft. You'll kiss your lover in the morning by writing before you go out into the world, and when you go out, you'll gather bouquets for your sweetheart by collecting fresh material from the call of a bird, the rattle of a streetcar, the odd accent of that guy on the cell phone, that unexpected phrase in the ad in the subway car.

You'll work at all this, because marriages aren't always sweet. Some days, you may hardly be on speaking terms. Some days, you feel your partner hates you or is cheating on you with someone else, maybe the fellow who just got a piece in the *New Yorker* or is merely in front of the mike in the neighborhood poetry slam. But you carry on. You fetch the groceries. You tuck your partner into bed at night and promise to dream together.

And out of this constancy — through tantrums and all — will come that blaze of creation when the sun shines at midnight, when time will stop or speed up for you, as you will when you are so deep in the Zone that no move can be wrong. Depending on your choice of theme and direction, you may find you are joined by other creative intelligences, reaching to you from across time and dimensions in that blessed union that another poet, Yeats, defined as the "mingling of minds."

When the sun no longer shines at midnight, when you are back on clock time, you won't waste yourself regretting that today you're not in the Zone. You are still married. You'll do the work that now belongs to the Work.

11. DANCE WITH THE TRICKSTER

The Gatekeeper is one of the most important archetypes that is active in our lives. He or she is that power that opens and closes

our doors and roads. The Gatekeeper is personified in many traditions: as the elephant-headed Ganesa in India; as Eshu/Eleggua
in West Africa; as Anubis in ancient Egypt; as Hermes or Hecate
in ancient Greece. I open all of my gatherings by invoking the
Gatekeeper in a universal way, with the request:

May our doors and gates and paths be open.

They say in Spanish, "Tiene que pagar el derecho" (You have
to pay for the right to enter). In many traditions, it is customary to
make an offering to the Gatekeeper when embarking on a project
or a journey. The offering required of us may simply be to check
in and show a little respect.

There is a close affinity between the Gatekeeper and the
Trickster. A being like Hermes or Eshu may play either role. One
of Hermes' appellatives, *stropheos*, literally means "socket," as in
the socket of a hinge that enables the pin to turn, and the door to
open and close. So we can think of him as a Hinge guy — as in
"hinge of fate" — or a Pivot. As he swings, so do our fortunes.
Hermes steps through the doors between worlds with a hard-on,
as men often transit from the dream world to the waking world
and as hanged men enter the afterlife. Hermes is penetrating, and
this is the effect of synchronicity. It pushes through, it opens up,
and it inseminates.

Trickster is the mode the Gatekeeper — that power that opens
doors in your life — adopts when you need to change and adapt
and recover your sense of humor. If you are set in your ways and
wedded to a linear agenda, the Trickster can be your devil. If you
are open to the unexpected, and willing to turn on a dime (or
something smaller), the Trickster can be a very good friend.

The Trickster will find ways to correct unbalanced and over-
controlling or ego-driven agendas, just as spontaneous night

dreams can explode waking fantasies and delusions. Our thoughts shape our realities, but sometimes they produce a boomerang effect. The Trickster wears animal guise in folklore and mythology, appearing as the fox or the squirrel, as spider or coyote or raven.

Anansi, a Trickster god of the Ashanti of Ghana, brilliantly and hilariously evoked in Neil Gaiman's novel *Anansi Boys*, is a spider and also a man. "It is not hard to keep two things in your head at the same time. Even a child could do it." He makes out that he is the owner of stories. Indeed, to make friends with the Trickster, we want to be ready to make a story out of whatever happens in life and to recognize the bigger, never-ending story that may be playing through our everyday dramas. If nothing goes wrong, it has been said, you do not have much of a story. The Trickster knows all about that.

We are most likely to meet the Trickster at liminal times and in liminal places, because his preferred realm is the borderlands between the tame and the wild. He invites us to live a little more on the wild side. He approves when we make a game or a story out of it when our plans get upset, our certainties scrambled.

He insists on a sense of humor.

The well-known psychic and paranormal investigator Alan Vaughan tells a great story against himself about the peril of taking signs too seriously. He read that Jung had noted a perfect correspondence between the number of his tram ticket, the number of a theater ticket he bought the same day, and a telephone number that someone gave him that evening.

Vaughan decided to make his own experiment with numbers that day in Freiburg, where he was taking a course. He boarded a tram and carefully noted the ticket number, 096960. The number of the tram car itself was 111. He noticed that if you turned the numbers upside down, they still read the same. He was now alert for the appearance of more reversible numbers. Still focused on his theme of upside-down numbers, he banged into a trash can during his walk home. He observed ruefully, "I nearly ended by being upside down myself." When he inspected the trash can, he saw that it bore a painted name: JUNG.

It was impossible not to feel the Trickster in play. Alan felt he had been reminded — in an entirely personal way — that the further we go with this stuff, the more important it is to keep our sense of humor.

A title of Eshu, who is both Trickster and Gatekeeper in the Yoruba tradition of West Africa, is Enforcer of Sacrifice. He is the one who makes sure that the gods receive their offerings. The price of entry may be a story, told with humor.

12. THE WAY WILL SHOW THE WAY

There is a practice in Ireland called *vaguing*, which Patricia Monaghan writes about beautifully in *The Red-Haired Girl from the Bog*. On a country walk, when you come to a fork in the road, you let your body choose which way to go. You will notice that a foot or a leg has a tendency to turn left instead of right, or the other way around, and off you go. Of course, this is practice for a day off, when you do not have anywhere in particular you need to be at noontime and you do not mind being off the maps.

Yet being ready to fall off the maps, and make an unexpected find when you do that, is practice for a kairomancer on any day, even when on a tight schedule. David Mitchell, the author of *Cloud Atlas*, found a new book was waiting to meet him when he got off a tram at the wrong stop. Mitchell relates that around Christmas in 1994, in Nagasaki, he got off at a wrong tram stop and stumbled upon "a greenish moat and cluster of warehouses from an earlier century." This was his first encounter with Dejima, a trading factory of the Dutch East India Company, built on a man-made island in Nagasaki harbor. For two and a half centuries, when Japan was closed to the outside world, this was the sole point of contact between Japan and the West.

Twelve years after alighting at the wrong tram stop, David Mitchell published his extraordinary historical novel *The Thousand Autumns of Jacob de Zoet*, which richly deserves its tremendous critical and commercial success. Mitchell succeeds in transporting us into the mental and physical worlds of two cultures at the close of the eighteenth century. He is a master of what he amusingly calls "Bygonese," conveying how people thought and talked in an earlier time in a way that never seems labored or antiquarian. Among his memorable characters, Dejima itself becomes indelible. And he found it by getting lost.

Antonio Machado says it with poetic clarity:

Caminante, no hay camino,
se hace camino al andar.

Wayfarer, there is no way,
you make the way by walking it.

[My free translation]

In my workshops, we often sing a song that came to one of my students, a writer from Minnesota, when I led a journey for members of an Esalen retreat to seek power songs, the kind that entertain the spirits and provide wings for shamanic travel. Some of the members of that retreat brought back very old songs in the languages of their ancestors. One brought back "Yellow Submarine." Some brought back original material. This is the liveliest of those songs, an anthem for kairomancers, imagineers, and sidewalk Taoists:

Make it up as you go along
Make it up as you go along

Make it up
Make it up
The way will show the way

When you get the hang of it, you let the original text go hang.
You pummel and pillow-fight with the words:

Make it up
Shake it up
Fake it up
Bake it up
The fox may know the way
The star will light the way
The dream will show the way
The heart will find the way
The way will show the way

THE OATH OF THE KAIROMANCER

Twelve rules for the kairomancer, and one OATH, which will
help us to remember the heart of the practice. To navigate by synchronicity and catch those Kairos moments, we need to be:

Open to new experience;
Available, willing to set aside plans and step out of boxes;
Thankful, grateful for secret handshakes and surprises;
    and ready to
Honor our special moments by taking appropriate action.

CHAPTER FOUR

THE BOOK OF
SIDEWALK ORACLES

"Things have a life of their own,"
the gypsy proclaimed with a harsh accent.
"It's simply a matter of waking up their souls."

— GABRIEL GARCÍA MÁRQUEZ,
One Hundred Years of Solitude

Sidewalk oracles are very much in business in Japan. At a
hillside shrine of Inari near Osaka, for example, people
come for crossroads divination. When you arrive, you make an
offering to request that the god Inari and attendant spirits — who
often appear as foxes — be receptive to your request for guidance.
You are given a cylindrical box with a hole in the bottom. The box
contains three long wooden rods, each carved with a number. You
are instructed to shake the box until one of the rods falls out. The
number one, two, or three will tell you who you are going to study
in what is about to become an exercise in people-watching.

You are now guided to follow a path to the back gate. From
here, you can observe people and cars moving along a road. Your
assignment is to pay close attention to the person whose number

came up — so, for example, if you drew the number two, your task would be to scrutinize the second person to go by. Which way are they traveling? On foot or by car, or on a bicycle? Alone or in company? Age, gender, dress? Every detail.

When she was researching a book on the popular cult of Inari, anthropologist Karen Smyers visited this temple to try this method of divination for herself. She drew the number one, so when she went to the back gate, she did not have to wait long for the oracle to speak. She heard it first, in the buzz of a motor. Then a man appeared riding a red motorbike. He passed from her right to her left and vanished around a curve in the road.

She carried her impressions back to the shrine, where she was dressed in a white vest, for purity, and admitted to an audience room dominated by an Inari altar flanked by two white fox guardian statues. She told the priest the question she had brought to the oracle: Would her research be published as a book? The priest listened to her description of the man on the motorbike. He faced the altar and prayed before playing speaker for the oracle. Yes, he told her, her book would be published because the person she observed was traveling toward the south, which was auspicious. Her aim would be realized quickly, because he was on a motorbike. The color red was a very good sign in this context, because the color red is associated with the god Inari. His fox statues are often dressed in red bibs, ready to be fed.

The consultation ended with payment of a modest fee. The priest's reading proved correct. Notice the simplicity of this practice. You set your intention, you invoke a greater power, and then you make it your game to study the first (or second, or third) person who appears on the road, with the frame of that sacralized intention. The purpose of going to a sacred place was to prepare the seeker to see something in the ordinary world in a sacred way.

Going to a special place in a sacred way may help focus your intention. The effort and expense involved in getting yourself there may create heightened expectations. The element of prayer and ritual and the evidence of past achievements will grow your sense of imminent revelation and may recruit unseen helpers. All of this will increase your energetic magnetism, your ability to attract the events and encounters that will answer your need for help or counsel.

Asking for help from friendly spirits is always a good idea. However, you do not have to leave home to do that. And you do not need to travel far to consult an oracle.

Oracles will speak to you where you live, through the signs and symbols of the world around you. To receive their messages, and join in the deeper play behind them, you need to remember that OATH of the kairomancer: be Open to new experience; Available, willing to set aside plans and step out of boxes; able to give Thanks for what the world gives you; and ready to take action to Honor what comes in a Kairos moment.

And here are the games. Games 1 to 15 are designed to start or make your day, and games 15 to 17 are designed for two or more players.

GAME #1. PLAY SIDEWALK TAROT

There are two basic ways to approach oracles. The first way re-quires you to set a theme or pose a question for the oracle. In ancient times, this often involved lengthy preparation and signifi-cant cost — ritual purification, animal sacrifice, payoffs to priests. Today you might go to a medium or a tarot reader. You might consult a preferred divination system you have learned yourself, casting runes, or coins for *I Ching*, or using tarot cards or cards from another oracle deck. You might do some book-dipping, opening a book at random and seeing what is in the text that is in front of you. You might take your question to your dreams by set-ting a theme for dream incubation. You might take your question to the world by agreeing with yourself that whatever pops up into your field of perception in a certain period of time will be a re-sponse from the oracle of the world to whatever is on your mind.

The second way is to let the world set a theme or pose a ques-tion to you. All this requires is being ready to receive, and allow-ing enough space in your mind and in the physical structure of your day, to notice what the world is giving you. The oracle may speak to you in the voice of a bird or a backfiring car or words overheard from a stranger. It may give you an image in the logo on a delivery truck or the pattern of clouds or the currents in water. It may appeal to your sense of smell, giving you a breath of perfume that connects you to a person at a distance, or a rank odor that tells you that something is rotten. In unsought, spontaneous ways, the oracle of the world may jab a message at you by giving you a repeated symbol or situation, coming at you again and again like a recurring dream, until you realize that you must figure out what is going on and *do something* about it since action as well as understanding is required.

You can play sidewalk tarot either way, by approaching the world with your theme or by letting the world suggest a theme to you. I started using the phrase "sidewalk tarot" after I noticed that things keep literally popping up, like tarot cards, on the streets and sidewalks of the small city where I live. Sometimes these pop-ups are actual cards, playing cards or business cards or cards from a children's game. Sometimes they are chalk drawings, in the hand of a child or members of a late-night college kids' stoop party. They may be abandoned books, left on the steps of a row house for anyone to take. Trash collection days are especially rich for pop-ups of this kind. A symbol or message may be presented by the logo on a truck or the letters on a novelty license plate or a poster that has blossomed in the window of the corner florist.

In fact, anything that enters your field of perception, through any of your senses, within your chosen time frame may count as a card in play, even as one of the greater trumps.

I played the drive-by version of sidewalk tarot on a day when I needed guidance on how to help a friend who seemed to me in danger of making some terrible mistakes because she was gripped by fear in relation to current challenges. I decided that I would receive the first unusual or striking thing that entered my field of perception during a drive to a meeting, as a response from the world to my question, *How can I help my friend?*

On a back road in green Vermont, I noticed a sign in front of a little white country church. The sign read, "Courage is fear con- quered by love." That was exactly the message my friend needed. In passing it on to her, I was able to open a deep and affirming conversation. Actually, the sign on that church is a message for all of us, every day. Courage is not the absence of fear. Courage is fear conquered by something stronger. Call it love.

A medical researcher I know plays the straphanger's version of sidewalk tarot on her commutes on the New York City subway.

One morning, rocking between tight-packed fellow commuters in a subway car, she noticed the text of a poem on a poster that appeared on the wall:

> Not incorrectly
> they advised me
> to use the long spoon
> if I went to dine with the devil.
> Unfortunately
> on those rare occasions
> the only one available
> was short.

The lines are from a poem titled "Precautions" by Eugenio Montale. The poster was part of a sponsored series titled *Poetry in Motion*.

The poem in the subway car gave a shiverish start to my friend's day. "I felt like the Devil card from the tarot was in play," she told me. In the course of the day, she had many experiences that made her wish for a long spoon. She felt that some of her work was stolen without attribution. She felt put down by her boss. She found herself thinking of the picture of the Devil in the old Rider-Waite tarot, where the chains that are holding humans hang lightly, hinting that they have choice; they do not have to remain in thrall to an oppressive situation or perhaps an addiction. They are only captive because they have told themselves they have no choice.

These reflections led the researcher to take a good hard look at the assumptions that were keeping her in what she felt was a toxic job situation. At the top of the list, not surprisingly, was the notion that she needed the money and would not be able to match her paycheck anywhere else. So she stayed at the meal table with a spoon that was too short until she was "let go," as they say, in a notably callous way, a year later.

The poem in the subway car is an example of how the world deals us cards of its own design that — like tarot cards — can be used for both reflection and divination.

Let's look at several simple versions of sidewalk tarot. As in drawing from a tarot deck, you can choose to play with as few or as many cards as you like. The big difference is that a tarot deck offers you only seventy-eight cards; the number of cards in the world deck cannot be counted.

Put Your Question to the World

Do you have a question or theme in your life on which you would like help or guidance right now? Then try to state that theme as clearly as possible. A simple way to do that is to fill in the blank in the following statement: "I would like guidance on _____." Your theme can be large or small. You can ask for guidance on your plan for next weekend, or a romance, or a possible job change, or what you are supposed to do with the rest of your life. Don't make a whole laundry list of themes. That confuses the oracle. Select one theme that has some real energy for you.

The game now is to be ready to receive the cards that the world will deal you. Just as you would clear a space on the table to spread tarot cards in a reading, make some space in your day. Decide on the time and space within which you will play. You might decide to play the game during the whole of your lunch break, during a walk, during your daily commute, or during ten or twenty minutes when you leave yourself free, in any setting you choose, to let the world speak to you.

You may decide to play with just one card from the world. This means that you are willing to receive the first striking or un-expected thing that enters your field of perception as an immedi-ate response to your intention for guidance.

You may choose to play with a three-card spread. This means

you will make it your game to notice three things in your environment and make a story out of them.

Or you may leave yourself open to any number of cards being dealt.

Let the World Deal the Cards

I find it is often more interesting to see what question the world is putting to me rather than putting my question to the world.

Here's how I play sidewalk tarot, almost every day. I make it my intention, the first time I leave the house (or wherever I am staying) in the course of a day, to gather three observations from my external environment. These do not need to be extraordinary in any way, just things that pop up on the street — a kid's chalk drawing on the sidewalk, the logo on a van, a dropped coin, an abandoned shoe.

Because I am highly visual, the first things that enter my field of perception are often things that I see. But they may be sounds that are irresistible or intriguing — the cawing of crows, a gust of a stranger's conversation, someone singing along with whatever is playing on their headphones. Sometimes my strongest impression comes through my nose. Sometimes it comes kinesthetically, like a Chicago wind that folds you in half.

DOG WALK CHRONICLES

When I journal my observations, I sometimes label these reports the "Dog Walk Chronicles" because so often sidewalk oracles appear when I am walking my little dog.

"Gotta try for the big one!" the cheery mother of a large family greeted me as we followed the path around the lake in the park on a late-summer day. Her gang had set up a veritable fishing camp: canvas foldout chairs, hampers, rods and reels, jars of bait, drinks and snacks. I had never seen anything big that has gills and fins caught in this lake, but then there are many kinds of "big ones" in life.

Walking back, I noticed that the day was starting to rhyme. A huge banner with a fish was hanging from a pole near the top of a brownstone on my street. It may have been there for a week or two, but now it captured my attention, blowing in the wind, insisting on the theme of going for the Big Fish. I smiled, remembering the wonderful film with that title starring Albert Finney as the master of tall and finny tales.

Further down the street, a young man was strumming a guitar on one side of a car, singing what sounded like an original, unfinished, composition. His girlfriend watched and listened from the other side of the car, which was full to the gills with clothes and boxes and bedding. They were moving in or moving on. A big day for them.

I returned to the park the next day and came upon an earnest fisherman, casting his line from a gap in the cattails at the western end of the lake. I asked him if he had ever caught anything here.

"Yessir. I just caught a bass as big as my tackle box. The biggest fish I ever caught in my whole life."

His tackle box was large and chunky. A bass that size would certainly be a Big Fish. I was skeptical about his fish story.

I wished him a good one and was almost at the other side of the lake when I heard him yelling. "Hey, lookit! I got one!"

He hoisted his rod high in the air, so I could see what he had caught. The fish was truly as long as his tackle box. He posed for a picture, then unhooked the bass and let it drop back in the water.

A snatch of Ovid returned to me: "Chance is always powerful. Let your hook always be cast; in the pool where you least expect it, there will be fish."

WHEN THE WORLD DELIVERED THE WORLD CARD

In sidewalk tarot, one card may be more than enough.

I was teaching a course in divination two hours away from my home. For the whole of the drive home, I reflected on the clear and simple reading one of my students gave me on the question I had posed: how to proceed with a certain book idea.

Once home, I walked my dog in the smaller of our neighborhood parks.

I glanced down and noticed there were two banknotes at my feet. One was a dollar bill, the other a twenty. The sum of the two was of course twenty-one dollars. A nice windfall. But I was thinking about more than the money itself. The number twenty-one has very special significance in tarot. Trump XXI is called the World or the Universe card. When it comes up in a reading, I see it as a powerful invitation to get out in the world and do your thing. In one deck that I use, the picture on the card shows a bold and beautiful naked woman dancing with a cosmic serpent. The message is: Get out there. The world is waiting for you.

I made the decision then and there to go ahead with a new book I intended to title *The Three "Only" Things*.

GAME #2. WALK A DREAM

Jung said that one of the things he liked to do with a dream was to "circumambulate" it, wander around it, considering it from many angles. He liked to do this while in physical motion, wandering around his house on the lake, through the garden, into the woods.

This is a grand way to get greater perspective on a dream. Walking with a dream for a while, you may find that more of the dream narrative returns to you. You are almost sure to get commentary of some kind from what you notice playing around you, wherever you happen to be going.

You may find that both inner and outer perceptions accomplish what a dreaming people of central Africa say we must do with a dream. Like other cultures that value dreaming, the Yansi of Zaire have special words for dreamwork practice. According to anthropologist Mubuy Mpier, the Yansi share dreams every morning, and the core of their approach to dream exploration is embodied in the term *a bumi ndoey*, which means to "turn a dream." The teaching is that we need to turn a dream carefully, as we might lift a great rock, to see what is underneath, on the side that is not initially visible.

It's not only a matter of letting the world illuminate the dream; it's a case of letting the dream illumine the world. "We do not always have only to sit with closed eyes, moving around in our heads, to draw closer to an image. We can put it in our pocket and carry it with us throughout days and nights," as Mary Watkins wrote in her passionate appeal for us to let images speak to us and through us. "You not only see different things, you see things differently" when you are seized by poetic imagery, poet and scholar Kathleen Raine observed.

One of the things we want to do when we are walking a dream is to notice when it starts to play out in the world around

us. There might be a considerable time gap between the dream
and its unfolding in the world, so patience and a decent memory
— assisted by your journal! — may be required. When a dream
does begin to manifest in external reality, let an alert flash on your
inner control panel. In my mind, the default version is: *Dream
Playing Out Now*.

When the dream starts playing out, you have several options.
They are not mutually exclusive. If there is no sense of danger
and the original dream left you feeling happy and confident, you
may be content to let the dream play again and enjoy it with all of
your senses. Maybe you'll find that a sense of "rightness" comes
with this: that you have made the right choice, that you are in the
right place, that at last you have found the right friend or lover or
teacher. If you had a darker sense of the dream — if it involved
risk or danger — you will want to be poised to change the script,
solve a problem, avoid that accident or that drama at the office.

As a dream plays out in exterior reality, you may notice that its
symbolism is now alive in your world. This can become a whole
education on how to refresh and renew our perspectives on what
is a dream and what is real. *We need to take dreams more literally
and waking life symbolically*.

A dream may be fairly literal in the sense that it reveals something that is happening or will happen in the future in the ordinary
world. Yet when the dream is enacted, we see that there is symbolism in the physical event. So a literalistic dream can point to a
symbolic play in the outer world. Let's consider some examples.

A man I will call Yves dreamed that his ring finger was cut off
in an accident. There was blood and pain, and he saw the splintered
bone, and woke with feelings of dread and fear. When he brought
the dream to me, I asked very early, as is my practice, whether it
was possible that he could lose a finger in a literal accident, maybe
cutting or slicing something. Did his work involve such risks?

Well, yes, it did. He worked part-time pruning vines on a hillside in southern France, where he lived. He agreed that he would need to be more watchful about how he handled the secateurs.

We proceeded to discuss the symbolic levels of the dream. Hard to miss the significance of losing the ring finger in terms of a relationship. He was not married, but he had a live-in partner and felt her interest had begun to stray. This brought in the Freudian bit. Did the loss of "tall man" — the middle finger — speak of a decline in sexual performance?

Yves walked with his dream. Within the week, it began to play out when he made a false move while working in the vineyard. He only narrowly managed to avoid cutting off his own finger with the pruning shears. It was the ring finger, as in the dream. The partial fulfillment of his terrible dream led him to confront the symbolic issues. He sat down with his partner. She told him, with the sexual candor for which the French can be notable, that she was dissatisfied with his sexual performance and had already taken another lover. They agreed to separate.

◆

I start the day by holding my memories of my dream adventures in my mind before getting out of bed. I want to be able to replay the best of my overnight movies. I am eager to harvest what can give guidance and juice for the day. Sometimes I want to dwell on details and bring back a full narrative report. Sometimes I am happy to let details fade and simply hold the heart of a dream, or a single thread I can pull to bring back the rest at another time or follow back through the labyrinth of the dream space. While many in our society are suffering from a dream drought, some of us are so prolific in our dream recall that we risk swamping ourselves with too much information. Less can be more.

When I have wrapped my head around enough of what happened in my night expeditions, I have a quick gulp of coffee before walking my little dog, who has been waiting patiently for me to return to his world. My dream will walk with us.

On a certain morning, I am excited and deeply stirred by a dream adventure in which I was in the situation, and seemingly the body, of a Royal Air Force pilot in World War II. I have known him, perhaps, since before my present life. As I pause for my dog to sniff a fire hydrant, I think about him, and a nurse that he loved, and what was going on in the dream. I feel a deep sense of communion with this man, who died before I was born. I feel that somehow I am present in his life and he is active in mine.

As on most days, I make it my practice to notice three new things in the two blocks we walk before we get to the big park. A license plate is often one of them. The one I notice today belongs to a registered nurse. This speaks to me. Over all the years I have been teaching Active Dreaming, the nursing profession has been the number one occupational group represented in my workshops. Nurses have so many practical applications for the techniques. It speaks to me again, even more strongly, because of the dream that is walking with me. The Pilot loved a nurse.

In the park, as we walk around the lake, I am simply open to what the world gives me. This morning, I nod to the beautiful weeping willow across the water. Her hair, which was green last week, is yellow and thinning as winter comes on.

I come home, grab a full mug of coffee, and sit down to type up my dream report and my notes on what I observed in the world around me. In my sidewalk tarot today, I did not notice any trumps. But there was a court card, for me, in the RN's license plate. Princess of Cups, perhaps. Or Princess — even Queen — of Disks.

Now I will do another everyday practice: getting guidance from a book. This may be called *bibliomancy*, literally "divination by the book." But today I am content with *stichomancy*, "divination by the line." I have already chosen the book. I am going back to Heraclitus, the pre-Socratic philosopher whose fragments tickle the cognitive brain and arouse and delight the imagination. I am using the translation, with extensive commentaries, by Charles H. Kahn. The book falls open.

I close my eyes and let my pointing finger decide which line will be the one for today.

I open my eyes. My finger is pointing at a fragment that reads in translation:

Gods and men honor those who fall in battle.

I'm not immediately thrilled. War and violence and bloodstained heroes. Oh dear. Yet I feel a deep sense of confirmation of the truth and importance of my dream, which took me into the life of a very brave man who was killed in a war. The line from Heraclitus deepens my sense from my dream that there is community between the dead and the living, between mortals and immortals: communion as well as communication.

I write a one-liner for the morning:

I am in communion with the dead. They are alive in me,
     and I am alive in them.

I write this again on an index card, in the fairest hand I can manage. I place the card in a deck of similar cards that contain dream summaries, thoughts for the day, and similar inscriptions.

GAME RULES FOR WALKING A DREAM

1. Carry a dream or image that has power or mystery for you as you go out into the world around you.

2. Let the world illuminate your dream. You can do this by making a selection of observations. See whether they relate to your dream, amplify it, or provide a kind of "second opinion" on the dream.

3. Let your image illumine the world. See how your perception shifts when you carry a certain image in your mind. You may notice that you look at different things, and look differently.

4. Be open to forgotten levels of the dream and unnoticed aspects and connections coming into sharper focus as you simply walk with the dream, without trying to figure out what it means.

GAME #3. KEEP YOUR SECRET BOOK

Your personal journal is the most important book you will ever read about synchronicity, as well as the most important book you will ever read on dreams, though you probably will not begin to understand just what a treasure chest it is until you have followed the practice of journaling for at least five years. Your journal is where you will record the clues and symbols the world around you and the world of dreams are giving you. It is the database where you will amass evidence of the objective reality of phenomena like precognition and telepathy. It is the chronicle where you will track the themes and symbols that recur in your life. It is the mirror that will show you where you tend to make the same moves, and perhaps the same mistakes, when your life loops around to a familiar choice or temptation, and where you manage to escape the tedious circle of repetition and rise on the spiral path of personal evolution. Your journal will become the best encyclopedia of symbols you will ever find. It will also become your very best book oracle.

Let's be clear. We are not talking about the kind of diary where you give yourself freedom to vent and moan and eventually (hopefully) write your way through a tough emotional path. A venting book of this kind has its uses. It can be great self-therapy. And the time will come when you will want to burn it, and probably should, letting the old stuff that it contains fall from you as the snake sheds its old skin.

We are talking about a book of secrets you will want to keep and consult for the rest of your life. It must be a secret book in a primal sense. It is your book. Nobody else gets to read it without your permission and your presence. If your partner insists on reading your journal, get another partner. There is a very instructive story about this from a writer whose entry into a marriage, and departure from it, were bookended by journal espionage. While engaged, she discovered that her fiancé was regularly spying on her journal and did not like what he read. She decided this was a test of her commitment to the relationship, that the price of a successful marriage would be to give up her essential privacy. She stopped journaling for a long time, still very uncomfortable about the prying man who was now her husband. She had to take it up again because it nourished her writing. Now she made sure that her journal was kept secure under lock and key. Then she found that her husband had found a way to read her journal again despite all her best efforts. This caused her to take a long, cool look at the relationship. She realized it had become totally airless and unfulfilling. She chose her secret book over her husband and got a divorce.

I like to travel with a journal-size sketchbook whose blank pages and quality paper encourage me to draw as well as write. I transcribe as soon as possible on my laptop, since my handwriting has become an unbreakable code, even for me, and I must type from the memory traces laid down by my hand on the page as fast as I can. Keeping my journals in electronic data files gives me an instant index, since I date and title each entry, and a search-engine function that enables me to track a symbol across decades in seconds.

Your personal aesthetics, writing style, and sense of safety will all influence your choice of journal. You may want a journal with archival paper and hand-sewn binding in a gorgeous leather cover. Like Hemingway, you may prefer a little Moleskine notebook that will fit in your back pocket or purse. You may be content for now, as you compose your life, to carry a student's composition book.

The key is to write something in your journal every day. When you remember a dream, you don't have to spend a second asking yourself what you will write. You just get it down, whether it is an epic narrative or a wisp. You date your report, you give it a title, you note your feelings, not only inside the dream but right after. You run a quick reality check, asking yourself, in particular, whether it is remotely possible that any part of this dream could play out in some way in the future, literally or symbolically. You add your first associations with key elements in the dream. You accept the research assignments the dream may have given you — to check the etymology of the Greek word for *truth*, to locate a "Newark Castle" that is not in New Jersey, to inquire discreetly whether that earring (not your own) that you dreamed you found on the bed might belong to another woman your partner has been seeing on the side. You decide on an action plan to bring guidance, energy, or healing from the dream into regular life — you'll go dancing, you'll paint a picture, you'll get the red shoes, you'll study the red otter. And, of course, you will walk the dream.

It was by keeping a journal for twenty years that Paul Kammerer developed his law of Seriality, a major point of departure for Jung as he developed his own theory of synchronicity. Kammerer started a logbook of coincidences when he was twenty, noting recurrence, or clustering, of identical or similar things in time or space — especially names and numbers. He defined *Seriality* as "a recurrence of the same or similar things or events in time or space" — events that, as far as can be ascertained, "are not connected by the same acting cause."

He noted "a quasi-gravitational attraction between like and like." Kammerer largely disregarded the inner side of synchronicity, so his theory is ultimately sterile and superficial; but his attention in logging his observations is admirable.

We can also be inspired by the practice of another dedicated journal keeper, the German polymath Georg Christoph Lichtenberg (1742–1799). He recorded thoughts, observations, and aphorisms, starting in his student years, in notebooks that he called his "Waste Books" (*Sudelbücher*). He borrowed this term from the English accounting houses of his day. For English book-keepers, a waste book was a temporary register of transactions, jotted down in rough form before being entered in meticulous copperplate in a formal account book. I like the throwaway quality of the term. It encourages us to get down the scraps and the rough sketches, without concern for form or structure or even spelling.

Lichtenberg's Waste Books are crackling with choice one-liners, such as "A person reveals his character by nothing so clearly as the joke he resents." We notice the same thing in the notebooks of Mark Twain, seething with "snappers" and "aston-ishers." We may be inspired to make the practice of composing or harvesting a daily one-liner part of our journal keeping.

As you play the many games described in this book, you'll find you never have a shortage of material for your secret book. You jot down the first novelty license plate you saw in a day, the first words you heard after leaving the house, the inner sound track you found was playing in your head — and maybe playing through you to the whole building — when you were in the shower. You record your one-liners, invented, borrowed, or stolen.

When you have plenty of pages, you'll come back to your journal to do bibliomancy, or book-dipping. Much more will soon be revealed, and if you are new to journal keeping, you will soon be kicking yourself for not starting one — or sticking to one — years ago.

Melody shares this personal example:

Meeting the Astronomer Seven Years ahead of Time

I kept dream journals starting in 1979. In 1990, I left many things in California with my parents, including my journals.

Years passed before finally I was able to retrieve them. I opened my journals again in 2004. I found this entry: "An astronomer in a bedroom with three baby beds and three infant sons. The man looks at me and says, 'I cannot come right now,' and gestures toward the beds."

I recorded this dream seven years before I met my husband, an astronomer with three sons from a previous marriage. I met my husband because I took the first job offered to me at a very low point in my life, after a big shake-up. I had gone to the university to apply for a job and found that there was a job available in astronomy. My background is in art, and I had never thought about astronomy, but I needed a job and took the one available — and met, and married, the astronomer with the three sons from the dream I had forgotten.

GAME #4.
LISTEN FOR YOUR DAILY KLEDON

"We are not deprecating!"

I am startled by this loud declaration, coming from a stranger in conversation with another man outside in the street. *Deprecate* is not exactly a household word. Since I am walking beside a church when I hear this snatch of conversation, I am drawn to reflect on the etymology of the word, which is connected to prayer and how we use prayer. In the original Latin, to *deprecate* is to "pray against" something, to pray it away. I take the message that we don't want to put our focus on what we oppose or seek to avoid, but on what we want to manifest in a positive way. I realize I now have my first one-liner of the day: "Don't pray *against*, pray *for*."

The first kledon of the day, like this one, is one of my favorite sidewalk oracles. As noted, the Greek word *kledon* refers to the first sounds you hear coming from silence — maybe a snatch of conversation, or the cry of a bird, or the sigh of wind in the trees.

Monitoring kledons was a favorite form of divination in the ancient world. At Pharai in the Peloponnese, there was a market-place oracle that delivered messages through sounds received in this way. If you were seeking guidance, you approached the statue of Hermes, the divine messenger, in the center of the walled market. You whispered your request for counsel in the rough-hewn ear of the god. Then you clapped your hands over your ears, shutting out the noise of the market, until you reached the outer gate. There you took your hands away from your ears, ready to receive the first sounds that came to you, as the response of the divine messenger, "the friendliest of gods to men."

In everyday life, the stir and bustle of a gritty city street may deliver a kledon as effectively as preceding silence, when a message becomes audible through undifferentiated white noise.

If you are interested in writing, sidewalk snatches of conversation can be like starter dough. Walking the street, I overhear this gust of emphatic speech from a fellow on his cell phone: "It took years of beating myself up to realize I can choose my path." Now *there's* a statement in which many of us could recognize ourselves.

On another city walk, I run into a couple of old guys on the sidewalk. One says to the other, "They took your world away from under you."

The second old guy, on a walker, responds: "Yeah, they took my world away."

"What you gotta do is tell everyone, like everyone."

"Or get a gun and shoot somebody. That's what I feel like doing."

"Forget the gun. Tell your story. That's more powerful."

Now *there's* a one-liner for any day.

The Call of the Rainbird

There it was again, the call of the rainbird. But this could not be. I had never heard this bird in any part of North America, let alone this urban park in the Northeast. It had to be someone whistling for his dog. The whistle changed, a happy dog with flapping ears materialized through the maples, and my guess was confirmed.

But for a moment, I had been transported back to another park, in Surfers Paradise, Queensland, where my parents retired. I walked a path there, slowly, with my father when I visited him before his death. He loved to hear the call of the rainbird and would imitate it perfectly, even after his stroke. The Pacific koel — as ornithologists and bird-watchers call this kind of cuckoo — derives its familiar name from the fact that it is often heard before rain and storms. The males are black with red eyes, and their calls in mating season are very demanding.

Strange and welcome, this vivid reminder of a scene from the other side of the world in the whistle of a dog walker. When I heard the rainbird, I was thinking about the content of a class I was leading that evening on "Partnering with Spiritual Guides." I was reminded that our spiritual guides include loved ones who have gone to the Other Side before us and that they can become extraordinary life counselors.

My father played a very direct role in healing old family wounds within days of his death. In the year that followed, my father visited me, and another family member, repeatedly. He confirmed the reality of life beyond physical death. He delivered messages for the family that helped us navigate life issues. In subsequent years, my father showed me some of his transitions on the Other Side and his eventual choice of a new situation where he would no longer be available for communication on a regular basis.

I thought of him now, with deep love and gratitude for playing the role of family angel in so many ways. And I thanked whatever inspired that other dog walker to make the call of the rainbird that day.

The Language of Birds

The most eloquent urgent kledons may be expressed in the language of birds. I have received very important messages in the voice of the red-tailed hawk, in the chatter of crows, in the hoots of owls, in the conversation of ravens. Sitting out on a deck in the foothills of the Cascades around midnight, I received a three-part weather advisory in three avian tongues. First came a strange, slurring graveyard cry, which I only later learned was a warning signal from a heron. Then came ten minutes of owls hooting. Then, for twenty minutes, a conversation that sounded far more interesting than any set of talking heads on television, wafting in from over the red cedars. That was the ravens, talking, talking. They were all speaking about the thunderstorm — relatively unusual in these parts — that was about to break.

Crows and ravens have a rich vocabulary. "Crows communicate their motivations, identities and report on local conditions each time they caw or croak," John M. Marzluff and Tony Angell explain in their excellent book *In the Company of Crows and Ravens*. "But sounds made by crows are much more than simple signals that we occasionally intercept. Together they encode a complex language, steeped in cultural tradition."

Alas, like most humans, I am often tone deaf to what the crows are saying, noting little more than the difference between a caw and a trill, or between a long caw and a short one, and the multiple cries of assembly and dispersal.

But one morning, I could not fail to notice the long, harsh caws of a lone crow perched in a linden tree across the street as I walked my dog back from the park. The crow sounded assertive, maybe territorial, but I did not know what he was saying until I started crossing the street. There, flattened next to the dotted yellow line, was a small gray-brown squirrel, freshly killed.

Sometimes messages are simple. The crow was saying, "Don't anyone dare to run over my breakfast again."

GAME RULES FOR
CATCHING YOUR DAILY KLEDON

The rules for catching your kledon of the day are very simple.

Be alert, as you go about your world, for the first sounds that come out of silence or out of the shapeless noise of a city street. This may be a snatch of conversation, someone singing along with whatever's playing through his headphones, the sound of an animal, the call of a bird.

When you are in a group, there is a variant of this game that had exceptional importance for the Greeks. When you are in a company that falls silent, the first sound or speech to come out of that silence may be more than a kledon. It could be a *hermaion*, the direct intercession of Hermes, the god who loves to intervene through seemingly natural events and everyday phenomena.

GAME #5. DO IT BY THE BOOK

It's been a popular form of divination for as long as humans have had writing and pages to write on that can be turned or shuffled. It probably began with casting pieces of wood on which designs (like runes or ogham script) had been carved. It's hard to imagine ancient Mesopotamian diviners shuffling stacks of hard-baked clay tablets covered with cuneiform script, but they may have practiced a kind of divination by lucky dip, reaching into a basket of such tablets.

We can begin to call this kind of sortilege *bibliomancy* (literally, "divination by the book") when we go back close to the beginnings of Rome, to the time of an ancient king named Tarquinius Superbus. He was approached by a wise woman, or sibyl, from the region of Troy. She said she had nine precious books that contained the secrets of what Heaven and Earth want to have happen in this world. She demanded a fantastic price for these books, which were not books as we know them, but a pile of loose pages, bundled together with ties. Some were inscribed on sheepskin, or goatskin, or tree bark, or thin strips of wood.

Incredulous at the price quoted, the king spurned the offer. The sibyl promptly destroyed three of her books. She told the king that the price for those that remained would be the same. This made him edgy, and some of his counselors turned pale at this strange bargaining process. But the king refused the new offer, and the sibyl promptly destroyed three more books. She declared that her price for what was left was the same. Now thoroughly rattled, the king called for the augurs to get a second opinion. They reported a prophecy that the kingdom would be offered a treasure that day but would suffer disaster if the gift were refused. The king now paid the fortune demanded for a third of the sibyl's secrets.

Or so goes the story. In it, we hear the echo of other stories of a book of the secrets of everything that appears and disappears, and washes up again in fragments, so that humans can discover only a part of the nature of time and the universe, of creation and destruction — which is just as well, since we know the human capacity for misusing knowledge that is power. In any event, the Sibylline Books became critical to world history. They were replaced several times. Under the empire, they were moved from the temple of Jupiter on the Capitoline Hill in Rome to a vault under the temple of Apollo on the Palatine Hill. An august college of secular priests, whose members had typically held high state office, were entrusted with pulling verses from the collection — as you might pull tarot cards from a deck — to perform a reading.

The Sibylline Books were most often consulted to get a second opinion on an anomalous event, like the flooding of the Tiber or the birth of a two-headed ram, but also to elicit the will of the gods on important undertakings and to receive guidance on what measures the state might need to take to propitiate the powers above.

In 405 CE, the master of Rome was a half-barbarian general named Stilicho who had been fighting a series of savage battles against Alaric and the Goths; Stilicho usually won, but at a ruinous price and without a clear resolution. He did not like his ratings from the Sibylline Books, which hinted that he was out of favor with the gods. He did what other men of power have done when they disliked the opinions of diviners and dreamers; he tried to shut them down, in this case by ordering the destruction of the Sibylline Books. Though the empire was now officially Christian, the culture of Rome was still deeply pagan, and this was widely viewed as an outrageous act of blasphemy that would bring punishment from the old gods.

Soon news reached Rome that barbarian hordes had crossed

the Rhine, heading for Italy. A cabal of disgruntled officers over-threw Stilicho; in 408, he was beheaded. Two years later, the Goths sacked Rome. There were many believers in the old ways who muttered, "I told you so."

A word about words. *Bibliomancy*, as noted, is literally "div-ination by the book." When the word entered the English lan-guage, it especially referred to divination by *the* book, the Bible. In Augusten Burroughs' memoir *Running with Scissors*, one of the characters engages in what he calls "Bible-dipping."

If you think that God, or a god, is going to speak through a book or a verse, then you choose the text according to your cultural values and religious tradition. For the Greeks, Homer's *Iliad* and *Odyssey* were favorites for sortilege; the Romans added Virgil (but liked Homer, too). For those of Christian formation, the Bible was the favorite book from the start and remains so in many neighborhoods. Abraham Lincoln was in the habit of opening his family Bible to get a second opinion on his dreams. In the world of Islam, the Koran has played the same role. In Persia, the collected poems of Hafiz or Rumi are hardly less valued as book oracles.

You can do bibliomancy with a sacred text, in which case you will probably want to approach the operation with respect and a degree of ceremony. You may feel, as the ancients did, that a larger power will speak to you through the book, guiding your hand and your eye to the correct passage, whether you have asked for guidance on a specific issue or have simply opened yourself to direct revelation. You may want to address a prayer or request to the agency you hope to provide a message through the book, as believers do when they turn to the Bible, the Koran, or the collected writings of someone they regard as a guru or spiritual master.

Among secular versions of bibliomancy, the Dictionary Game is perennially popular. This will give you a word for the day — and maybe many further clues among the warren of definitions and etymologies.

You can take a breezy, casual, even promiscuous approach to doing it by the book. You might play with whatever book comes to hand, at home, in a bookshop or library, or on the road. This is my own everyday approach. I think the shelf elves enjoy it. Certainly, it brings them out to play. Arthur Koestler spoke of the Library Angel, a bookish spirit that produces the right text at the right time. In Hebrew angelology, there actually is a library angel, though I have never invoked him by his Hebrew name. When I speak of the shelf elves, I am talking about a lesser and lively fraternity of book-loving spirits who can be credited or blamed, among other things, for the book that drops from the shelf, or flies open suddenly, or turns up on top of a pile at the used bookshop or among the new arrivals at the library, and may have a hand in what turns up when you open a book at random in quest of a flavor for the day or a comment on a theme.

I am fairly sure that a shelf elf was at play in the experience of the poet Robert Browning when he sought guidance on his infatuation with Elizabeth Barrett. Browning decided to reach for a book blindly and use whatever his hand lighted on for his divination. He was disappointed when he found that he had snatched up a copy of an Italian grammar. What possible guidance could he hope to find here? He decided to play the game anyway. Opening the grammar at random, he found himself looking at a text for a translation exercise that read as follows: "If we love in the other world as we do in this, I shall love thee to eternity."

Maybe an agent of Eros was moonlighting as a shelf elf that day. Browning and Elizabeth Barrett married, and their union was one of the most creative unions in the history of literature.

While writing this chapter, I was actively engaged in an online forum where my students were sharing dreams and experiences of synchronicity. I was struck by how overlapping elements were appearing with growing frequency in their reports, as if members of the community were interacting in their dreams and synchronistic experiences in their inner and outer worlds. I reached, without looking, into a shelf near my desk and pulled out a fairly hefty book that proved to be a volume of Jung's correspondence. Fine. I opened it at random and could almost hear Jung's voice as I read the opening lines of a letter he sent to a lady in England in 1942:

My dear Mrs. Crowley,

Your dream of June 26th — the Arab — has anticipated
several of my dreams this month, in which I was in Africa,
I myself wearing a long shoka [something like a long white
shirt].

Jung is noting the resemblance between, and possible interweaving of, his own dreams and writing and research preoccupations and the dreams of one of his admirers. He is also talking about precognition, without the caution he often evinced on that subject in formal presentations. He goes on to say that a second dream report that Mrs. Crowley sent him also seemed to "anticipate" his own dreams and discoveries.

While engaged in extensive and sometimes frustrating home renovations, Meredith survived what she had feared could be a difficult conversation with her carpenter. She now picked a book at random from a big pile of books waiting to be placed on bookcases that had not yet been finished. The book in her hand proved to be Marshall Rosenberg's *Nonviolent Communication*. It fell open to the statement "Empathy Lies in Our Ability to Be Present." She reflected that in their meeting, her carpenter had spontaneously displayed more empathy than she might have expected, telling her, "If it were my project, I would want it to be the way I had imagined it." She had responded in similar spirit: "I'm so grateful for all the hard work you've done to make it nice." Meredith reached the conclusion that "the theme of the book and the one-liner it gave me brought home how we can transform potential conflict into a mutually satisfying outcome through heart-centered intention."

You may want to pick a favorite book or author for consultation for a while. You'll not only get messages; it's a grand way to become more familiar with a text and to view it from different angles. Favorite books I have used this way include the *Odyssey*, Emerson's *Collected Essays*, Yeats' *Collected Poems*, Herodotus' *Histories*, and Coleman Barks' exquisite renderings of Rumi.

On one of my trips, I turned to Rumi for my morning messages. These are the passages that leaped to my eye on three consecutive mornings:

Day 1:
Your real country is where you're heading,
not where you are.

Day 2:
When you're traveling, ask a traveler for advice,
not someone whose lameness keeps him stuck in one place.

Day 3:
We've come to the presence of
the one who was never apart from us.

I was so keen on Rumi in that period that I dubbed my morning book-diving "Rumi-nation." However, my favorite books for everyday bibliomancy are my personal journals. As you will discover once you become a long-term journal keeper, your private journals become the best encyclopedia of symbols you will ever read and much, much more. When I open an old journal at random, I often find, in a dream report from years before, clues to a situation that is manifesting in my current life. I am reminded of connections with other lives and parallel worlds and with gods, spirits, and others. I am sometimes given necessary pause when I read about an episode in my earlier life that is repeating now; the players and setting may be different, but the key issues — the opportunities, challenges, or temptations — are much the same. This gives me motivation to consider whether I want to proceed on a circular path of repetition or choose a spiral path, which is the way we go when we recognize that we are somewhere we were before but can now make more enlightened choices.

GAME RULES FOR
PERFORMING EVERYDAY BIBLIOMANCY

1. Set a theme for guidance, or simply be open to what the book will reveal. Your call.
2. Choose a book, or by reaching at random into a shelf, let the book choose you. (The book — maybe with the help of a shelf elf — may already have chosen you, popping up in an unlikely or unmistakable way. If so, go with that.)
3. Open the book at random.
4. Close your eyes, and let your fingers choose which part of the text, on which of the pages that are now open, is going to speak to you.
5. Consider the chosen text carefully. What are your first feelings and associations?
6. Feel free now to forage forward and backward around the selected text and see if there is more for you there, but don't blur your focus on the first lines that came up.

GAME #6. PLAY WITH SHELF ELVES

Shelf elves can be active assistants for the Muse. A gifted young Canadian novelist named Sheila Heti was a guest on my radio show. Preparing for our conversation, I read a short novel Sheila had written called *Ticknor*, which is basically a dialogue between the divided selves of the biographer of the famous nineteenth-century American historian William Hickling Prescott, author of *History of the Conquest of Peru*. I found myself in a curious time loop reading this spare and elegant work, since I was reminded — for the first time in many years — that Prescott was one of the historians I chose to study in my historiography course as a senior honors student at university in Australia.

I asked Sheila on the air, "What on earth got you interested in Prescott and his biographer?"

She explained that before she had any thoughts of Prescott, she was waiting for a friend in a coffee shop. The friend was delayed. To fill in time, she reached at random for an old book on a shelf of used books for sale. Her hand seized an elderly volume with gold leaf on the binding. It was Ticknor's biography of Prescott. She opened the book and found herself fascinated by the voice. She could hear the man behind the words. She purchased the book, took it home, and — after a creative lag of several months — it triggered her novel.

Shelf elves are often at play in my preferred bookshops, which tend to be quirky independents and havens of twice-sold tales. One of these haunted establishments is just down the street from my home, which is a mixed blessing because in the course of a year, a significant portion of this bookshop's stock migrates up the street, into my house.

It was in this bookshop that I found the meaning of a funny dream word (*chantepleure*) in a book placed at eye level from my point of vision at the door, so I could not fail to see it, and was thereby drawn into transtemporal intrigues involving a poet-prince of Orléans in whose name Joan of Arc went to war.

It was here, over the holidays, that I repaired with the feeling that there was something of Jorge Luis Borges' that I urgently needed to read that day. Newly arrived, casually dropped on top of a short stack in the literature section, was an English translation of *El libro de arena* (*The Book of Sand*), which I naturally purchased. I opened this collection of Borges' later stories and was immediately engrossed in a tale ("The Other") in which Borges meets a much younger self on a bench. Borges tells his younger self what life will bring him over the forty years that divide them. The young Borges, who believes he is dreaming, will forget the information he has received from his older self, letting it fade like a dream. This tale wove together two of my favorite themes, the many varieties of the double and the relativity of time, and I was inspired by it to write a story that was published in my collection *Here, Everything Is Dreaming*.

Sometimes I turn to the shelf elves for a second opinion on a dream, as I did when I woke from this scene:

BATTLE OF THE TURTLE AND THE CROCODILE

There is a commotion outside. I go to the window and see an army is encamped along the edge of a body of water where a battle is taking place between a giant turtle (the size of a dozen men) and a giant crocodile. I call to the others to come and see. When I turn back, I see that the army has saved the turtle, which is being transported to safer waters. They have constructed or opened a kind of raceway, and the turtle is swimming between walls. Now I see that there are actually two giant turtles.

I look out to the water again. Beyond military lines, the

crocodile stands on a headland, tail raised like a scorpion, apparently triumphant for now. I understand that the conflict will be resumed. It's part of life. The role of the army is to ensure that neither party destroys the other.

I woke from this dream feeling both excited and satisfied. In the dream, I was an observer. I felt that I was being shown something of huge importance in life.

I know both Turtle and Crocodile as members of my personal mythic bestiary. I have swum with sea turtles, and I am from a country famous for crocodiles. I know that in life, there are contests between opposing forces and attitudes that must continue if life itself is to go on.

Instead of spending much time in analyzing the dream, I made a quick drawing and decided to ask Jung for a second opinion. Who better? I had already had it in mind to do my daily bibliomancy with Jung's *Memories, Dreams, Reflections*, a book of seminal importance in my life and the most personal and accessible of his works. However, when I reached into the Jung section in a glass-fronted bookcase in my personal library, the shelf elves had other ideas. Another volume in Jung's *Collected Works* came flying off the shelf, striking me lightly on the chest.

Naturally, I changed my ideas about where to look for guidance and took this flying book to my desk. Its title is *Two Essays on Analytical Psychology*, which seemed to match the revelation of the two turtles in my dream rather nicely. The volume is a dual edition of two of Jung's early essays, volume 7 in the *Collected Works*. I opened the book at random and read this:

There is no energy unless there is a tension of opposites; hence it is necessary to discover the opposite to the attitude of the conscious mind.... Repressed content must be made conscious so as to produce a tension of opposites, without which no forward movement is possible. . . . Just as high always longs for low and hot for cold, so all consciousness, perhaps without being aware of it, seeks its unconscious opposite, lacking which it is doomed to stagnation, congestion and ossification. Life is born only of the spark of opposites.

I saw that there was no need to invent a snapper to carry the essence of my dream. Jung had given me one. *Life is born only of the spark of opposites.*

This little incident is a practical example of how we can turn to a book to give us a second opinion on a dream. Our curiosity may, of course, take us far beyond the initial passage we find when we open a book at random. I found myself drawn, irresistibly, to read both of the essays in that volume of Jung, in which we find his mind devising and developing theories of aspect psychology, the shadow, and the relations between the ego-self and the collective unconscious, which were to become fundamental to his approach.

The Magnet in the Book

Sometimes, beyond the play of the shelf elves who make books and papers appear and disappear, I sense other minds and other hands. In the last stages of writing this book, prowling the night, I found my copy of Yeats' *Autobiography* off its shelf, on a table where I had not placed it. There was no occult reason for this; it had been moved, with a small pile of other books relating to the poet, as part of a housecleaning.

I accepted the invitation to revisit Yeats' life through his words. Opening the book at random, I found myself reading a lively chapter on his mixed relations with the Irish mystic, artist, and writer George Russell, who used "AE" as his pen name.

The next morning, I opened another book in that pile. It is a collection of occasional pieces, mostly literary and art criticism, by AE, titled *The Living Torch* and published by Macmillan in 1938, that I found in a used bookstore near Mount Vernon in Washington State a couple of years before. I had placed it in my forest of books without examining it closely.

This was evident, because when I opened *The Living Torch* at random, I found five loose pages hidden inside the book. They are written in a fine lady's hand from an earlier time. They are fair copies of five of AE's poems. The lady who made these copies was meticulous. She noted the publication date (1926) of the edition of AE's *Collected Poems* from which she borrowed the lines she copied and the numbers of the pages where these poems may be found.

I sat very still as I read the poem on the top page. It is titled "Magnet," and it begins as follows:

I had sweet company
Because I sought out none
But took who came to me,
All by the magnet drawn.

The timing of this discovery was perfect. Within the previous week, I had borrowed a line from AE as a section title in chapter 3 of this book: "Your own will come to you." The theme here is we draw people to us magnetically. I did not know that AE had written a poem on this theme until I opened the old book I had acquired and forgotten.

The later part of his poem, I must note, develops a darker tone. It seems that AE (described by Yeats as first and last a "religious teacher") is reflecting, ruefully, on an affair of the heart that tempted him to set aside the austere spiritual discipline he imposed on himself. I wonder whether, in her secret heart, the unknown copyist was stirred, by her recognition of herself in a similar drama, to make "Magnet" her own by putting it in her own hand.

GAME RULES FOR PLAYING WITH SHELF ELVES

There are no game rules for playing with shelf elves. You let them start the game and make up the rules as you go along.

GAME #7. CHANCE AN ENCOUNTER

The *Book of the Road* (*Putnik*) was on a list of banned books in
tsarist Russia. It was a treatise that attributed high importance to
chance encounters. It reflected traditional beliefs about whether it
is lucky or unlucky to meet certain kinds of people on the road. To
meet a nun, a priest, or a blind man is unlucky. To meet someone on
a bridge or threshold is ominous. Such views were deeply rooted in
traditional Russian culture, even in the mind of tsars. Ivan the Terrible thought it was a terrible omen if anyone crossed his path when
he was setting out on a journey, and he had such offenders killed.

I am more in sympathy with the Greek saying that the gods
love to travel in disguise, so we should take care of strangers.

"Mind attracts mind." Jung observed that this principle is at
work in chance encounters where more than chance seems to be
involved. Jung described what happened when a stranger — a
general — sat down next to him on a train:

> We talked, and although he did not know who I was, he
> told me all about his dreams, which is certainly unusual for a
> man of his position. The general considered that his dreams
> were absurd, but after listening to him, I told him that one
> of his dreams had changed his whole life, and that otherwise
> he would have been an intellectual.
>
> The general was startled and looked at me as though I
> were a witch, or at least a person gifted with second sight.
> But in reality, it was the unconscious which was knowing
> and directing. The general had sat down next to me because
> he was unconsciously searching for an answer.

Jung felt the general was called to sit next to him because
something deeper than his conscious mind was calling for a mentor, to help him make his dreams conscious.

My friend Carol, a family counselor and addictions counselor of great wisdom and compassion, encountered an elderly man who was praying for an angel.

Carol went to a pharmacy to pick up a prescription. There were some problems with the paperwork, and she was feeling quite grumpy. When she came out into the parking lot, she noticed an elderly man pushing a shopping cart, unsteadily, toward his car. When he reached his car, he left the cart by the trunk, still filled with his purchases, and slumped into the driver's seat, leaving his door open.

"I knew something was wrong," Carol told me. "I sat in my car as three people walked past the old man. Then I knew I had to check on him."

She walked over to the old man and said, "Do you need some help?"

"Did you ask me if I can use some help?" The man seemed incredulous.

"Well, yes. I did ask if you could use some help."

"You're not gonna believe this. Right before you showed up, I was sitting here praying to God to send me an angel. Could you put my shopping in the trunk for me?"

"I would be happy to do that."

The old man popped the trunk, and Carol loaded his shopping bags. The contents felt soft. Carol guessed the bags contained products like Depends, for older people whose bodies are failing. She noticed a walker, folded, and two canes in the trunk.

"I came out too soon," the old man told her when she had finished loading. He did not explain exactly what this meant, but he told Carol that he was the caregiver for his wife. They were both ninety years old, and they had been married for seventy years.

"Are you sure you can drive home safely?" Carol asked.

"I'll be okay. I know there is an angel watching over me."

Carol commented later, "If I was an everyday angel for him

in that parking lot, he was a kind of angel for me. I felt happy and blessed by this encounter. All my grumpiness was gone."

Chance encounters may not be *caused*, in the sense of being made by appointment, but they may be *called*.

◆

Chapter 5 of this book, "On Other Planes," is a narrative of chance encounters playing out at airports and on airplanes, in the midst of my frequent travels around the world. For me, the conditions of air travel are almost ideal for chance encounters with strangers. People are on the move — which may help release them from routine inhibitions — and at the same time, the circumstances are contained and relatively "safe." Contact need last no longer than the flight or the wait at the departure gate. Under these circumstances, strangers are often drawn together to commiserate about delays or share travelers' tales. Many will feel an active desire to tell and listen to stories, if only to shorten the seeming duration of a flight or a layover.

I do not initiate conversation unless I have a positive feeling about the person sitting next to me or am intrigued by the title of the book they are reading. Often my neighbor on a plane will be the first to speak, especially when I am carrying one of my own books. I will never forget the matriarch who took the seat next to me after settling her extended family in various parts of the airplane cabin. She noticed the beautiful cover of the second edition of my book *Dreamgates* and asked if she could look at it. Naturally, I handed it over. Opening the book at random, she found herself reading a section headed "Designing Your Home on the Other Side."

She turned to me in high excitement. "Is that really possible?" she demanded.

"Absolutely."

I explained the group adventures I lead, in which we have observed how the creative imagination constructs living environments — and cities, universities, and pleasure domes — on the other side of physical death.

"I will buy this book as soon as possible!" the elegant matriarch declared. "I have spent twenty-five years creating a jewel of a home in Carmel, California. I am going to be spending a lot longer in my next residence, and I want to get it right."

When strangers ask me what I do, I often say to them, "I am a storyteller, and it is my pleasure to help people find the bigger stories of their lives, and live those stories, and tell them so well that others want to listen."

To break the ice in conversation with a new acquaintance, I will often ask them to tell me a story. "What kind of story?" is a frequent response. To which I will then say, "Any story you like, from any part of your life." Everyone has a story that wants to be told.

Synchronicity and Significant Others

When synchronicity brings you into an important encounter with another person, you can be pretty sure that in some sense that person is going to be a significant other — partner, lover, spouse, soul friend, workmate, fellow traveler on the roads of life. Synchronicity may play matchmaker in arranging the first meeting or may come into play within an existing connection to show you that it goes deeper than you knew. You meet someone by chance, and you know that in some sense this was meant to be. You meet someone in an ordinary way, but then synchronicity comes into play, and you know this relationship is going to be far more than it seemed. Someone steps out of your life, and someone new steps in, maybe at the same place, even at the same time.

I know a woman who agreed to break up with her partner of many years and drove him to the airport. When they stopped for gas, there was his best friend, newly arrived in town, filling up at the next pump. The ex-partner introduced his friend to his now former partner. A week later, they went out for dinner. A year later, they were married.

"When two people meet synchronistically," Jean Shinoda Bolen wisely observed, "each person is 'a significant other,' and both are at a critical personal juncture and capable of being deeply affected, then dramatic changes can result." One of my students tells this story:

Because He Returned My Wallet

I met a significant other because he returned my wallet. He found it on the street after it fell off the roof of my car (isn't that where everyone keeps a wallet?), and used the information on my driver's license to contact me. I followed my intuition and offered to buy him dinner as a reward. We dated for two years, and this changed my life in many positive ways.

Very often the special moment that brings you together with a new love and/or an old soul friend involves recognizing that you already know each other, most likely through a dream. "I dreamed about my ex," an artist friend in Colorado reports, "a week before he walked into a meditation class I was attending in Boulder. Our eyes connected, and — zap! — there went nine years of my life."

You may or may not remember the details of the dream. Sometimes, however, a dream of Mr. or Ms. Right initiates a soul quest; you are on the lookout for the person you dreamed. Sometimes you have specific clues that will lead you to that person. Sometimes you must let things work out by a different logic.

Charles told me this story of an unexpected find that led him to pursue a relationship that flourished:

THE OLD WEDDING RING CONFIRMS A NEW DATE

I was debating whether to continue seeing a woman I met online. Because she lived on an island, I felt the ferry and traffic commute would be too cumbersome. I resolved to call her and let her know I needed to cancel our next date. I reached into my laptop bag to get my cell phone. Instead of the phone, my hand chanced on something cold, small, and rather weighty. I pulled this mystery object out and was amazed to see it was my old platinum wedding ring. It had been missing for over five years, and it chose that very particular moment to resurface!

Inscribed on the inside of the ring was my old anniversary date. I stood, stunned, for a moment and then realized the inscription matched the birthday of the woman I was ready to cancel dinner with! I took it as a clear sign that something was afoot; so I went out with this lady again based on that mysterious event. It's a year later. I now live with her, and we are deeply in love.

Sometimes being prepared for a chance encounter involves stepping decisively out of an old pattern, as in Joyce's story:

TEARING UP THE OLD PICTURE
AND STEPPING INTO A NEW ONE

After an eight-year on-again, off-again, long-distance relationship, I knew I couldn't go on with it anymore. I tore up pictures, and correspondence from and of him, in an effort to end the relationship once and for all, psychically and symbolically. Soon afterward, I dreamed of a tall, blondish man

walking out of the ocean onto the shore. A few weeks after
that, I had a chance encounter with a tall, blondish man. We
have now been happily married for more than twenty years
and have a tall, blondish son.

In today's world, chancing an encounter for romantic reasons
is a game that often begins by looking for a match on an internet
site. There are books to be written on how Kairos and the Trickster play in that environment. Here I will content myself with one
story, from a writer named Diane, about how synchronicity saved
her from opting out of an online dating site just before Mr. Right
showed up.

No Long-Distance Relationship

After much disappointment and annoyance, I decided to remove my profile from an online dating site permanently. I
went online to that site and noticed I had just received an
email from a man who had seen my profile. I checked out his
profile, and he seemed really nice. I decided to give him a
chance. When I noticed he lived three hours away from me,
I made just one change in my online profile. All I deleted
was the statement "NO LONG-DISTANCE RELATION-
SHIPS" — which, as it turned out, he had not noticed, lucky
for me. Then I replied to his email. We have been happily
together for four years, and I moved from New York to live
with him in Rhode Island. So this is no long-distance relationship.

Khalil Gibran counsels, "Think not you can direct the course
of love, for love, if it finds you worthy, directs your course." This
is another open secret, for romancers as for kairomancers.

GAME RULES FOR CHANCING AN ENCOUNTER

1. In the presence of another person, scan your own energy field. See if anything in you has shifted in the presence of that person.
2. Check for a sense of déjà vu and any resemblance between this person and situation and remembered dreams.
3. See what memories from your own life come to mind in the presence of this person.
4. Trust your feelings!
5. If you feel comfortable and have established common ground, see what happens when you ask the new person to tell you a story.

I suspect that all these rules can be successfully applied to internet dating games, but since I have never played those, I can only counsel you — if that is your scene — to try them out and see what happens. *Bonne chance!*

GAME #8. NOTICE WHAT'S SHOWING THROUGH A SLIP

It's a game I find fun and helpful almost every day: *notice what's showing through a slip*. By playing this game, I found a dream editor and the wonderful publishing house that has brought this book, and five before it, into the world. I told the story in the acknowledgments to the first of my books published by New World Library, but it belongs here as well.

I had just devoted an hour on my radio show to the theme of "three 'only' things," the notion that we have three wonderful resources for guidance and everyday magic that we tend to dismiss as "only" this or that, by saying (for example) that a dream is "only" a dream, or that a moment when the universe gets personal is "only" coincidence, or that a flash of inspiration is "only" imagination.

The show went very well, and I had a strong urge to reach out to someone in publishing immediately and propose a book on this theme. When I picked up the phone, I intended to call a senior editor at a major New York publishing house with whom I had worked before. On a sudden instinct, I looked up the number for an editor with a smaller house on the West Coast.

Her name was Georgia Hughes, and she was the editorial director for New World Library, an independent publisher based in Novato, California. Up to this point, I had communicated with Georgia only by letter and email. First contact was made when she approached me for an endorsement of a fine book on Celtic tradition, Frank MacEowen's *The Mist-Filled Path*. Later I had emailed Georgia to advocate Wanda Burch's beautiful book *She Who Dreams*.

I did recall a dream from many years before in which it seemed that a woman called Georgia — who appeared in an American Indian setting but was not herself Native American — was playing a very important and positive role in my publishing life. I found the number for New World Library. A robot voice guided me through the in-house directory, which eventually revealed Georgia's extension. I punched it in, expecting to get voice mail. After all, she was the editorial director of the house, and such people tend to be very busy and not often — if ever — available to first-time callers.

Georgia answered her own phone and greeted me warmly when I said my name. She spoke to me as if we were old friends, referring to a recent phone conversation.

"Excuse me," I interrupted, puzzled. "We've never spoken on the phone, though we did trade some pleasant emails."

"Of course we've talked on the phone. You told me about your vacation."

"Do you know who this is?"

"Absolutely! You're Robert Moss. You're the author we are publishing."

"That is amazing. I'm calling to discuss a book you may want to publish, but in my reality, you haven't even heard about it yet."

There was a short pause on the phone. Then Georgia realized she had confused me with another author, Richard Moss.

I refused to hear her apology. "There are Freudian slips, and then there are cosmic slips, and I love what this slip may be telling us. I'm calling to explore whether you might want to publish a book that involves coincidence — including how we can get guidance from slips and apparent screwups. And you start our conversation by telling me you know absolutely who I am and that I am the author you are publishing. What could be cooler than that?"

We had a lively conversation about dreams and coincidence

for half an hour, at the end of which time I promised to send Georgia a formal proposal the next day. I stayed up all night to pull it together. The time is always Now. Could you resist going with a slip like that? The book that resulted was *The Three "Only" Things: Tapping the Power of Dreams, Coincidence & Imagination.* I realized that my dream from years before, of a "Georgia" in an "American Indian" setting was indeed a rehearsal for my new publishing relationship when Georgia Hughes told me she is from Indiana. I continue to be enormously grateful for Georgia's slip on the phone, and for her extraordinary gifts as editor and friend.

◆

A word about Freudian slips. Freud gave his most complete account of the phenomenon named after him in his book *The Psychopathology of Everyday Life*, published in 1901, a year after *The Interpretation of Dreams*. It is a collection of essays that was probably better known and more widely read in Freud's lifetime than any of his other works. In my favorite local used bookstore, a shelf elf placed a copy of an elderly Macmillan edition, with A. A. Brill's translation, in my line of sight. The paper label on the spine had rubbed nearly away, like the label on a well-soaked bottle of wine, so I had to pull the book off the shelf to see what was facing me, which begins to sound like a Freudian joke in itself.

The merits of Freud's study of slips of the tongue and memory lapses are threefold. First, he assigns *meaning* to incidents that many of us tend to overlook. Forgetting the name of a town where you once stayed, or giving the wrong name to someone you know perfectly well, isn't simply a memory lapse or passing confusion; it speaks of something in you and your life situation that merits close attention because you can learn from it. Second, Freud does dreamwork with these incidents, applying the same principles of analysis to episodes in waking life as he applies to dream symbols. Third, his prime lab rat, first and last, is himself. Like Jung (and unlike lesser scientific minds who fail to realize that knowledge is state specific), he knows that understanding begins with self-knowledge and that the most important data on inner events (and their interplay with outer events) must be gathered from firsthand experience.

We follow Freud down some interesting trails as he studies such phenomena as forgetting names and otherwise well-known phrases, and word substitution. He recounts a chance encounter with a fellow traveler on a train who begins to quote the famous line, in Latin, in which Queen Dido of Carthage issues a terrible curse against Aeneas, the hero who loved her and left her: *Exoriare aliquis nostris ex ossibus ultor* (Let someone arise from my bones as an avenger). In the days when a good education still required Latin, Freud's educated companion would be expected to get the quotation right. But he cannot recollect the harmless indefinite pronoun *aliquis*. By the end of a long conversation in which Freud guides his travel companion through the free-association process he also applies to patients' dreams, they understand that there may be deep significance to the suppression of a seemingly harmless pronoun. In *aliquis*, the speaker now recognizes the echo of *liquid* and *liquefaction*. This reminds him that he's alarmed that his girlfriend may have missed her period. He's scared that he is the "someone" who will be cursed if he abandons his girl and a baby he doesn't want.

Now we come to the defect in Freud's approach to Freudian slips, which he called *Fehlleistungen*, meaning "faulty actions" or "misperformances." He wants to insist that word amnesia and name substitution are related to "disturbing complexes" that prompt the psyche to seek to repress memories and information that may cause us pain. We hear of a man who simply cannot remember the name of a business partner who stole his girlfriend and married her; he just doesn't want to know. Freud can't remember the name of a town he knows well (Nervi) when treating a neurotic, at a time when he himself is feeling nervous and may be heading for a migraine.

While Freud's theory of repression may apply to some of his examples, there's both more and less going on with our slips and memory lapses than he allows for. Common sense tells us that memory gaps can be the result of all sorts of life factors, from fatigue to drug or alcohol abuse, to migraine, to information overload. Einstein once made people laugh because, asked for his phone number, he had to look it up in the book. He declared that he had so much on his mind that he didn't need to burden it by adding the need to remember things he could easily look up.

I am generally pretty good with names, so when I call someone I know by a name that isn't their own, I pay attention to what may be showing through my slip. In one of my workshops, I kept calling a man "Michael" though I was perfectly well aware that his name was Don. Finally, I asked, "Who's Michael?" Through tears, he explained that Michael had been his partner for many years; Michael had died, but Don felt him close and was actually wearing his sweater that day.

On the Wrong Page

Typos can be a terrific source of insight. My friend Ana (one of those rare people who virtually never make spelling mistakes or commit typos) sent me an account of her experiences on a morning when she was running late and driving very fast. She was compelled to brake suddenly several times when cars in front of her stopped unexpectedly. Each time this happened, though frustrated because of her urgent need to get to an appointment, she noticed that the car in front of her had a novelty plate with an interesting message. More interesting to me, as I read her report, was that every time she described how she was forced to stop, she spelled "brake" as "break." "I was forced to break." "I was forced again to break." I commented that, for me, this would be saying loud and clear: it's time to take a break. That could mean slow down, get some rest. It could also mean break with your regular habits and patterns; break with your ordinary reality; be ready for a reality break, even for Eliade's "rupture of planes."

Had Mark Twain been able to notice a recurring typo, and harvest the message, he would have avoided bankruptcy at the high tide of his life as a bestselling author and beloved lecturer. I discovered this story when I was given the huge first volume of the recent edition of his unexpurgated *Autobiography*. Half this material is new to the public because Samuel L. Clemens (the author's real name) decreed that it should remain secret for a hundred years after his death, thus ensuring that people would be gossiping about him long after he was gone. Opening this tome at random, I found Clemens expressing his opinion, with exquisite clarity, on what he would like to do to one James Paige: "*If I had his nuts in a steel trap I would shut out all human succor and watch that trap till he died.*"

Who was the James Paige who brought out this savage desire for revenge in Mark Twain? Paige was an inventor with an idea for a typesetting machine. He convinced Clemens that his invention would revolutionize the newspaper and publishing businesses and earn the bestselling author a fortune far beyond his literary earnings.

Clemens always hoped to make a bundle doing something other than writing or speaking. He thought he saw his chance with Paige's plan for a typesetting machine. Remembering his sweaty days as a "printer's devil," toiling with heavy trays of type in hick print shops, he also dreamed of being present at the creation of a new technology that would make printing speedy and accurate.

Paige talked a good story. As Clemens ruefully recalled, Paige "could persuade a fish to come and take a walk with him." The author was soon convinced that Paige's machine was going to be the biggest thing since Gutenberg, and he drained his bank accounts to become the biggest investor in the project. However, the enterprise was bedeviled by delay after delay, costs rose, contracts were revised, and soon Clemens had sunk $150,000 into a project he had been assured would not cost more than $30,000. By the time Paige had completed a working prototype, his machine was obsolete, overtaken by new and superior typesetting machines. Clemens, the main investor, was left on the edge of bankruptcy.

Mark Twain could have avoided all of this pain and loss had he noticed what's in a spelling mistake. He simply could never get the name of the inventor right. Whenever he wrote to Paige, or about him, he misspelled the name, leaving out the *i*. I've gone through his correspondence and his journal entries on this theme. Again and again, he wrote "Page" instead of "Paige."

Mark Twain had decided to invest all his money in a machine that promised to make printing more accurate. Yet he could never spell the name of the machine or its inventor correctly. We might notice the dreamlike symbolism of leaving out the *i*. The whole wretched enterprise left out the author's *I*, his self-interest.

The Walking Dead on Wall Street

I was given a very strong warning about approaching financial disaster through a slip involving National Public Radio. The Wednesday before the collapse of Lehman Brothers, which set off the financial crash of 2008, I was driving to an evening class I lead for advanced students. I had the car radio tuned to the local NPR station. It was broadcasting the *Marketplace* program, a business report I don't often monitor.

Halfway through the show, the announcer said, "Now we'll do the numbers," meaning that they would give a summary of activity on the stock exchanges.

What followed was unexpected, inexplicable, and certainly never explained on that station.

Instead of a wrap-up of what had happened on Wall Street, I found myself listening to a complex skit. The plot involved mad scientists who were mass-producing zombies in the swamps of Louisiana, to make a fortune for a corporation that planned to market a new product called Zombie Gone in supermarkets all over America.

This was mildly entertaining, but by the time it was done, I was still waiting to hear the market summary. The program ended with no explanation as to why its time had been claimed by the walking dead.

Bemused, I shared this incident with my circle of dreamers. I speculated that it was telling me that Wall Street had been taken over by zombies. If that was the case, then what action should I take? Should I sell the modest investments in my retirement portfolio?

By my own logic — as someone who habitually navigates by synchronicity — the message was quite clear: Sell all stocks. Do it now.

But even I was unready to take such a radical step on account of one bizarre episode of a radio program. By the beginning of the following week, it became abundantly clear that I would have done well to have followed the logic of synchronicity. By the end of that week, the value of the stocks I own had sunk to 50 percent or less of what I had paid for them.

I did not panic. I was buoyed by a dream in which I was driving a high-performance car that took a nosedive, barreling down a one-lane road where a turn was impossible, in a near-vertical descent — until things finally leveled out and I came to a gentle rolling stop in what looked like a fabulous duty-free area at an airport. This encouraged me to stay in the market, and things eventually recovered.

◆

There are slips I do not want to correct because they give a smile and expand our understanding of something. More than fifteen years after I introduced my Lightning Dreamwork process under that name, most people who use it still write "lightening" rather than "lightning." I have not only given up on correcting them; I have decided I no longer really want to correct them. Through our kind of dreamwork and story swapping, we bring through light, and even some enlightenment, and we encourage each other to lighten up, a condition for flight.

Then there are the slips that turn linear thinking into pure poetry. A friend announced in a post online that she was writing a memoir in which she was describing a set of life experiences "in chronological order." A spell-check imp turned "order" into "rodeo." This made her laugh as she reflected how some of her life transitions had been like riding a bucking bronco. I suggested the one-liner "The deepest order is a rodeo." Heraclitus reincarnated as a cowboy. We don't want to mess with poetry, or miss a good laugh. And spell-check imps can cast spells.

GAME RULES FOR NOTICING WHAT'S SHOWING THROUGH A SLIP

Pause in the presence of a slip to ask what it might be showing. A slip of the fingers can be quite as revealing as a slip of the tongue. Don't correct or brush away typos without taking at least a quick look to see what they might reveal.

Don't be too quick to tag a slip as "Freudian." A lot more might be going on than Freud recognized.

GAME #9. CHECK YOUR INNER SOUND TRACK

Do you check your inner sound track, as you wake and at other times during the day? Do you notice how this can set the mood for the day, for good or otherwise? Do certain songs, popping up in your mind, connect you to certain people, life themes, or memories? Do you find you sometimes need to change what's playing inside your head?

In a dream, I am leading a group up my street. We are laughing and singing the old Cole Porter song "Wake Up and Dream." As we sing, the streets get wider, and the houses become more elegant and sparkle with magic and mystery as well as seasonal good cheer. Now the street is like a boulevard in Paris in festive season.

I woke with the song still playing in my mind, feeling deep joy and confidence. Context: we sang that song in one of my private circles earlier that week. Its magic in the dream reminded me that we want to check what's playing on our inner sound track — and change the tune when necessary.

When I suggested this exercise to a group of my friends and students, we very quickly had a fascinating community playlist, complete with liner notes.

Julie reported that she woke up that morning with the lyrics "Preacher says that when the master calls us, he's gonna give us wings to fly." They are from Josh Ritter's song "Lawrence, KS." Julie decided, "I'll take wings to fly with me for the rest of the day."

JoAnne reported that often she finds she has the same old favorite playing in her head as she enters the day — "Oh, What a Beautiful Mornin'" from the musical *Oklahoma!* She does not feel that the needle is stuck in the groove. "The song reminds me to look for the beauty in every day."

A Turkish artist commented that she checks frequently and often finds that subconsciously she has been playing a sad song. "I then try to change the music because I don't want a sad song to become my theme song for the whole day."

A Swedish bodyworker recalled, "When I was having a rough time in my life, I woke up with 'Shining Star' by Earth, Wind & Fire. I never wanted to listen to that group, but that day I received wind and fire to help get me through."

A woman in Texas contributed: "I wake up with different music every day. Today I woke up with 'Shake It Off' by Taylor Swift. In the dream, I was watching a sad news story on television. I have not heard that song in a long time. I took it as a message to keep a good attitude during the day, focus my attention on positive things, and shake off the bad stuff coming through the TV."

A Vancouver dreamer sent me this: "Today I accept the song that was with me when I woke, and I will let it play all day. 'Calling All Angels.'"

The song on your inner sound track may connect you to another person in your life, maybe someone at a distance. Wanda told me that a song she used to sing for her son when he was very small will still pop into her head when he is thinking of her and getting ready to call or visit her. The song is "He's Got the Whole World in His Hands." She smiles when it starts playing on her inner sound track, remembering the joy of slapping hands with her little boy as he tried to reproduce the words.

For several years, the song that connected me to one of my daughters was "The Banana Boat Song." We had so much fun with it, especially since my daughter sang the phrase "highly deadly black tarantula" as "highly deadly black *triantula*." I never corrected her. Instead, I encouraged her to make drawings of the Highly Deadly Triantula, which she depicted as a horrible fuzzy wedge with waving legs. When we were apart and I heard that Harry Belafonte cry "Day, me say day…me say day-o!," I would smile, knowing what was coming next: the deadly triantula and contact on some level with the daughter who created him.

When you check your inner sound track, don't just listen to the music; find the words that may or may not come with a tune. Check for voices from the past that may be cheering you on or bringing you down. Catch yourself when you start going over and over old histories of failure or regret, belittling yourself, telling yourself what's wrong with you in a way that cannot help you to be right. You may notice that an inner voice has been repeating things like "I'm such an idiot," or "I'm in so much pain," or "I'll never be able to face that crowd (or that person)."

Your inner sound track may include a whole chorus of voices of people who have lifted you up or pulled you down. Don't let all of them speak! Choose the ones you are willing to hear.

Above all, check your personal mantras. These are codes for connection and manifestation. These are the magic words that can deform your life or open up avenues of bright possibility. You may have borrowed some of your personal mantras from a spiritual teacher, or a favorite book, or one of those oh-so-cute boxes in your Facebook newsfeed. I have nothing against feel-good affirmations and statements of spiritual correctness, *as long as they work*. This means that they come to mind when you need them, when you need to respond to a challenge or make a choice at a crossroads. It means that they are playing on your inner sound track before you hit a Select button.

When you check your inner sound track, you may find that your personal mantras include:

- "I'm sick."
- "I'm fat."
- "I'll never meet the right guy."
- "I'll never have enough money."

There's no need for me to expand the list. You are going to make your own. When you detect a negative mantra of this kind on your inner playlist, you can try to delete it but may find that it comes back. You can try to override it with happy tunes and feel-good affirmations. I find that sometimes the best tactic is not to try to cancel a long-playing blues number right away, but to trip lightly around it, saying and singing better numbers.

Walking my dog in the park one morning, I checked my inner sound track and found I was engaged in making an inventory of the complaints in my aging body, all featuring pain. The pain in my dodgy knee, the pain in my shoulder, the pain of inflammation in one of my toes, the possible beginnings of a sore throat.

I hit my inner Pause button. I did not try to deny that my body was expressing these complaints and might need to be acknowledged. We don't want to push away what may be part of our body wisdom, or — in my case — my body crying out for a little TLC. All I did was to shift my attention to the dappled light among the beech trees, the gentle breeze stirring the surface of the lake and playing with my hair, the happiness of my little dog as he nosed after new smells and the nether parts of other dogs. And I said to the wind and the sun and the trees, "Thank you. Thank you for the gift of this day. I am grateful to be able to walk among trees, by water, with a dog who loves me no matter what. Thank you for the gifts and the challenges of this lifetime."

The best answer to inner naysayers and whiners may be to say to the universe: *Thank you.*

GAME RULES FOR CHECKING
YOUR INNER SOUND TRACK

1. First thing, on waking, check whether you have a song playing in your mind or a phrase or odd word that has lingered from a dream.
2. In the shower, check what you are singing or might feel like singing.
3. At different moments of the day, pause and ask yourself, *What is playing in my head now?*
4. If you don't like what you are hearing, try to delete that track from your playlist. If this is not so easy, choose a different track, something happy and light.

◆

As I complete this section, I notice that what is playing in my mind, uninvited, is "He's got the whole world in his hands." And I feel that marvelous sense of rightness, of being in and with a world where the love and protection of greater powers are always available, called or uncalled.

GAME #10. DÉJÀ VU ALL OVER AGAIN

You have been there, seen that, before the moment it plays out. A curl of hair falls across her forehead, just so, and you know you have been together before. You see the facade of that hotel, and you know the woman in the red dress is about to walk out on that balcony.

Déjà vu ("already seen") is when you have the strong sensation that something unfolding around you has happened before. It opens windows into huge questions: What is time? What is the self? What is normal? Where do our memories come from? Is there a real distinction between past, present, and future? Have we lived before? Have we already lived in the future?

Raven, one of my students, tells an entertaining story about this kind of experience. She was walking toward a conference hotel with colleagues. The woman in front of her told her male companion that she was getting a sense of déjà vu.

The man dismissed this, telling her that déjà vu is just "a hiccup in the brain."

Listening in, Raven was irritated but said nothing. However, she herself was now getting the sense that she had been in this scene before and knew what would happen next.

"I have a sense of déjà vu, too," she announced. "In a moment, a woman in a red dress will walk out on that balcony through the second door on the left." A few seconds later, the woman in the red dress walked out onto the balcony from that door. The man who said that déjà vu is just a hiccup in the brain turned very pale.

Déjà vu is probably the most common type of psychic experience. In surveys, 75–92 percent of normal subjects (in the United States, the United Kingdom, and Japan) report having had this experience. A recent survey of 444 students at three German

universities showed the incidence of déjà vu was very high —
over 95 percent — and a significant number reported having several experiences of this kind every month.

Our reactions to déjà vu can run the gamut from near-
paralysis to cold chills, to the impression that reality is being re-
booted, to a blessed sense of rightness and confirmation. I asked
some of my students to contribute their personal experiences of
déjà vu, and the range of feelings reported is fascinating:

- "Often my experiences of déjà vu bring a nearly overwhelming feeling of being known and held. In my thir-
  ties, I glimpsed a piece of furniture — in a certain light,
  at a certain angle — and this triggered a recognition of a
  childhood dream. I understood then that I was intended
  to be exactly where I was at that exact time. Consequently,
  it allowed me to be more in wonderment in the moment."

- "When I experience déjà vu, I usually first feel nervous,
  agitated deep, deep inside because what is going on is
  very different than a normal situation. Then I start to get
  curious. My mind gets active, and I start searching for
  how I can recognize what is going on around me. Soon I
  am engaged in a mental journey to find the source of this
  déjà vu. Sometimes this leads me to remember a dream
  or vision. Sometimes the source of the déjà vu remains
  mysterious, but I am grateful for it."

- "The feeling immediately alerts me to the potential importance of the situation or person. This may come with a
  sense of urgency, that some action is required. Acting on
  that sense, I was once able to save someone's life after he
  had a stroke, by being poised to rush him to the hospital
  in time for treatment."

- "When I have the sense of déjà vu, it's accompanied
  by the feeling that I'm in the swing of things. There's

positive resonance. I paid a lot of attention to déjà vu as a child. As I always seemed to notice it when things were flowing well, it became a sign of positive magic for me."

Why do we use a French phrase for an almost universal phenomenon? The phrase *déjà vu* was first used in this context by a French psychic researcher, Émile Boirac, in 1867. It was seized on by his contemporary, an even greater investigator of the supernormal named Frederic Myers, who carried it across the Channel in 1895 and gave it a home in the English language, preferring it to his own coinage, *promnesia*. Myers found the phenomenon of déjà vu of exceptional interest in his life's work, which was to establish the scientific validity of supernormal states and expand our definitions of what is normal to include and explain psychic and spiritual phenomena.

Myers addressed the question of how we know what we feel we know when we experience déjà vu. He speculated that this kind of knowing may arise from heightened subliminal perceptions of the external world and also from telepathic communication with other minds. We may be picking up the thoughts and memories of others. He suggested that déjà vu could be the upsurge of ancestral memories, especially as we visit the lands of our ancestors. It could also be the surfacing of buried memories of past experiences, triggered by emotion: "Almost any mental tempest may bring remote impressions to light — as storms will wash up cannon-balls on a long-since bombarded shore."

Then, of course, there is the matter of dreams. Myers wrote in his book-length essay "The Subliminal Self" that "a suddenly evoked reminiscence of a past dream may give rise to the feeling of 'déjà vu,' of having witnessed the actual scene at some indefinite time before.... The really important question is whether the connection may be other than casual, whether the dreamer may in some super-normal way have visited the scene, or anticipated the experience, which he was destined afterwards to behold or undergo."

We speak of *déjà vu* ("already seen"), but often the experience may better be called a case of *déjà rêvé* ("already dreamed"). Maybe you dreamed an incident before it manifested in the physical world. You may have forgotten the dream completely, but as it starts to play out, you remember something. By my observation, the dream self is forever tracking ahead of the ordinary self, scouting challenges and opportunities that lie in the future. Its expeditions leave trace memories of the future that come alive when we enter a scene we have dreamed.

Another of my students, now a teacher of Active Dreaming in Texas, reports this experience:

THEY SAID THAT BEFORE

I recall having a vivid déjà vu experience when I was at a bookstore coffee shop, studying for a college class. I recall two women walking in and sitting at the table next to me, having a conversation. I had the experience of everything coming into the present moment, of knowing what they would say next. But then it went further for me, and I began to actually see my dream playing in fast-forward on my inner screen. It was this experience that let me know that déjà vu comes from dreaming something before it happens.

For some, the experience is so strong that they feel they have entered a scene they have lived before in the physical sense, perhaps in a previous life. One of the most famous fighting generals in U.S. history, George S. Patton, is a notable case. In his American life, Patton had never visited Langres, a small town in northeastern France, until he arrived in December 1917 to take command of a tank school. But he declined the offer of a local liaison officer to show him around the town, once the site of a Roman military camp. Patton assured his liaison that he knew the place well because he had been to France before — as a Roman legionnaire. He led his own tour, pointing out the sites of the ancient Roman buildings and the place where Julius Caesar had once made his camp. Patton said later that he felt "as if someone were at my ear whispering the directions."

The prodigious Charles Dickens wrote a vivid account of an experience of déjà vu with the uncanny quality of *déjà vécu* ("already lived"). He is describing an incident on the road to Ferrara, in his travel book *Pictures from Italy*:

> At sunset, when I was walking on alone, while the horses rested, I arrived upon a little scene, which, by one of those singular mental operations of which we are all conscious, seemed perfectly familiar to me, and which I see distinctly now....If I had been murdered there, in some former life, I could not have seemed to remember the place more thoroughly or with more emphatic chilling of the blood; and the mere remembrance of it acquired in that minute, is so strengthened by the imaginary recollection, that I hardly think I could forget it.

This is the kind of déjà vu that we may indeed be inclined to call déjà vécu. It comes with the certainty that you know a scene because you have lived there, fully and completely, in a previous time. This recognition generally comes with strong emotion, though it may be bittersweet nostalgia, or a sudden afflux of joy, even exultation, rather than Dickens' "chilling of the blood." Dante Gabriel Rossetti captured the sense of someone or something "already lived" perfectly:

You have been mine before, —
How long ago I may not know:
But just when at that swallow's soar
Your neck turn'd so,
Some veil did fall, — I knew it all of yore.

You walked that cliff, you kissed on that bridge, you fought on that field of battle. You are sure of it. Maybe specific memories begin to stir. And there are more questions. Are your memories the revival of a forgotten episode from earlier in your present life? Are they ancestral memories, of members of your lineage or your spiritual kin who loved and struggled in the place you are at? Are they memories of a previous incarnation of your own spirit? Most interesting among all the possibilities: Is your sense of déjà vu triggered by recognition of a situation you have encountered in a *parallel* life that is now converging or overlapping with your present one?

While déjà vécu involves the sense of remembering the past — maybe a past lifetime or historical era — déjà rêvé often involves the sense of remembering the future. A dream that is playing out in the world now can be recognized as a memory of the future.

So we may have a great deal to learn and to gain by studying the phenomenon of déjà vu and being poised to ask the right questions and obtain the right navigational guidance next time we experience it.

Before I lay out some game rules, let me offer a cautionary tale, paired with an encouraging one.

The cautionary tale is one of déjà rêvé. On this occasion, I had a complete and exact record of a dream in which I entered a strange triangular building. I took the elevator to a certain floor, where I was met by a friendly man coming out of the restroom. He led me into his office, asking whether I would like anything to drink, such as "Coffee, tea, double scotch?" His office looked very strange to me, narrowing to a point like an elongated slice of pie.

I recorded the dream in my journal but forgot it until many months later, when I was invited to visit a powerful publishing executive in New York City. His office was in the Flatiron Building, which I had never entered before. As I looked at the exterior of the building, I knew I had been here before. When I got out of the elevator, a friendly man coming out of the restroom greeted me warmly, asking if I wanted something to drink, such as "Coffee, tea, double scotch?"

Inside the office, which narrowed to a point like a slice of pie, I lost it. I was so fascinated by the exact matchup with the dream — whose details all came back to me — that I completely failed to take advantage of my opportunity to have a free-ranging conversation exploring many options in my writing and publishing life. I was wooden, uninventive, going through the motions, half-paralyzed by that strange fascination. At the end of more than an hour, I am sure, my host had no idea why I had come.

The moral for me (and perhaps you) here is: when déjà vu starts playing (and a dream starts playing out), *don't freeze!*

The more encouraging tale I want to recount here involves reaching back into a dream, as it begins to play out, for survival information. Over early-morning coffee with friends in Bucharest, I recounted some fragments from a dream. A key character looked like Zbigniew Brzezinski, the Polish American former national security adviser. In my dream, I was trying to ship something and found it would have to be sent via Washington, DC.

My early morning flight from Bucharest to Warsaw, en route to the United States, that day, landed me in airport hell. Flight cancellations, fogbound airport, a huge crowd of edgy people from the former Soviet republics without Schengen visas, unhelpful airline staff at Warsaw's Chopin airport who seemed to speak only Polish. A man in the crowd complained on behalf of the stranded passengers. He looked like a dead ringer for the young Zbig Brzezinski. I now realized that I recognized the whole scene — the Ukrainian protesting at the desk, the nice Canadian girl who loaned me her cell phone when I found that mine had no service, the wait at an isolated baggage carousel to pick up bags when we were finally told we could not leave that night.

I reached back into the mostly forgotten dream to find a way through the mess. I remembered that in the dream, I could only ship something important via DC. At this point, the important thing I wanted to ship was myself! DC was not on my schedule, and there was no one at Warsaw airport with whom I could talk about a radical change of itinerary. But when I finally got to Frankfurt the next day, I was able to do a fancy shuffle and secured the sole available seat on a flight to Washington's Dulles airport, getting to the departure gate just before they ended the boarding process.

GAME RULES FOR MONITORING DÉJÀ VU

GAME SETUP

1. Record all the experiences of déjà vu you can remember.
2. Note what followed each of these episodes.
3. Discuss this subject with friends and colleagues, and ask them for their own experiences.

GAME MOVES

1. Be ready for your next experience of déjà vu!
2. Trust your feelings for immediate guidance.

3. Ask whether this could be a dream that is manifesting, and if so, see whether that brings up more details from the dream that you can use for navigational guidance.

4. If this feels like a "past life" memory, or a glimpse of a parallel life, see whether you can pull up more information about that life, and consider where you want (or do not want) to go with that connection in your present life.

5. Note what follows your new experience of déjà vu, in waking life and in dreams.

GAME #11. EXPECT THE UNEXPECTED GUEST

The best-loved of the Sufi poets, Jalaluddin Rumi, helped inspire this game. The purpose is to take a close look at some of the moods and feelings that turn up at our door, like unwanted guests, and distract us from what we are trying to do and that can even crush the joy and the juice out of us. "Negative" feelings that surprise us may range from impatience or anxiety to rage or fear or guilt. Yet we can also be diverted or swamped by feelings that have a better reputation — like empathy or pity — if we can't contain or channel them.

Rumi gave the general idea in a poem titled "The Guest House." Here, I am borrowing from the fluid version of Coleman Barks. In Rumi's poem, each of us is like a guesthouse where visitors are turning up at all hours, and we need to be ready to receive them in appropriate ways. These visitors are moods and feelings:

> This being human is a guest house.
> Every morning a new arrival.
>
> A joy, a depression, a meanness,
> some momentary awareness comes
> as an unexpected visitor.

Rumi's counsel is to "treat each guest honorably. He or she may be clearing you out for some new delight."

The game goes like this: Imagine yourself at the door of your house — your actual house or the house you would like to live in. Either way, this is also a guesthouse where visitors can appear at any time. Now picture that a feeling or experience that challenges you is at your door. You are going to open the door, and *name* that feeling, and inspect it in the animate or personified form in which it presents itself.

Next and most important, you are going to figure out what you want to do with this visitor. Just sending it away is unlikely to work; the feelings you deny will find ways to haunt you and steal your energy. On the other hand, with certain feelings — especially certain forms of fear, the mind killer — the best strategy (contrary to Rumi) may not be to bring them right inside the house, but rather to set them in a kind of "holding area" and call in help to deal with them.

You may, of course, find something at your door that you are not willing to allow to cross the threshold. Your ex-boyfriend may show up. Or something so charred or dirty you don't want it in the house. Or something you feel quite sure does not belong to you and for which you are not required to assume responsibility. We are not required to receive all callers. But we will want to deal with them, one way or another.

The first time I played this game in one of the workshops I lead, I met Impatience as the visitor at the door. He looked like a young, overstuffed, pompous version of myself in a power suit, so full of himself he really thought the world should make way for him every time he wanted something. I didn't care for him at all, but I made it my game to show him into a comfortable den, got him to take off his coat and loosen his collar, loaded him up with good books and good movies on DVD, and encouraged him to enjoy everything that was available to him while he relaxed and allowed the events he was waiting upon to unfold naturally.

A woman in that group met Empathy at the door. Empathy looked like Kwan Yin, but her form was entirely composed of water. The challenge was to engage with her without being swamped with emotion to the point of drowning. During our journey (aided by drumming), the woman succeeded in finding effective containment and channels for all that water of emotion.

In another group, a woman met Regret in the form of the man she had loved when she was nineteen. They sat down on a love seat. He spoke of his heartbreak when she left him. She explained that she felt she had no choice, because she had dreamed — all those years ago — that their life together would have been cramped and poor, and it was best for them to go their separate ways. She felt a bittersweet peace settle between them.

Other players have met and named a host of personal demons, including the "noonday demons" of Depression and Despair. Among the host: Anxiety, Guilt, Remorse, Anger, Self-Pity, Sorrow, Self-Importance, Resentment, and The Dominator (note the dominant definite article). In handling such unwanted guests, the guesthouse managers have followed various strategies. One player filled her house with music to soothe and cheer Remorse. Another met a strung-out Anxiety at the door and got him washed and cleaned in the shower and comfy in a fluffy robe. Sometimes other residents of the guesthouse came forward to help, Joy overwhelming Fear or Grief.

In the games so far, I have not yet heard anyone, except myself, name one of the trickiest demons, the one the desert fathers called Acedia ("ah-SEE-dee-yah"). This is the most deadly of the tribe of noonday demons, a dry dementor that sucks the juice and joy out of everything. Acedia is the demon of Not Caring. He is so tricky that at one point, he succeeded in getting the learned editors of the *Oxford English Dictionary* to declare him "obsolete" while snickering behind his cupped hand, "I'll be baaaack." Next time he shows up at my door, I'll see how he needs to be handled and will report back — assuming I succeed and therefore still care.

GAME RULES FOR
MEETING THE UNEXPECTED GUEST

Picture yourself looking from inside toward the front door of your home or the place where you are staying. Imagine that the doorbell rings or there is a tap on the door.

Don't think you know, for sure, who or what is there.

It may be the embodiment of a feeling or a fear. It may be someone long gone from your life. It may be the form of a challenge or issue you have preferred not to think about. It could be something or someone entirely welcome, but chances are that even so, you are going to have to get through some edgy moments.

What are you going to do?

Do you invite the guest right inside your home?

Do you let it into a confined space that will be a kind of holding area?

Do you turn the visitor away? Do you refuse to receive an unwanted message and tag it "Return to Sender"? (Sometimes this works; sometimes it leaves something unresolved that will show up later on.)

Be sure you give a name to your visitor.

Journal your experience at the end of the encounter and ask whether there is something you need to do, based on this encounter.

GAME #12. LOOK FOR THE SPIRAL QUESTION MARK

I have a little plastic figure of Anubis that I like to carry around with me. Anubis is the canine-headed god of ancient Egypt who is most closely associated with dreaming and travel between the worlds. He's the one you want with you, in friendly mode, at the gates of the world-behind-the-world. In early Egypt, children were given figures of Anubis as guardians of the night and as encouragement to dream strong.

The fact that my favorite Anubis talisman is just a five-dollar toy from the children's section of a museum shop tickles me and brings a warm fuzzy sense of connection with both my Boy Roberts and the big black dog I loved fiercely. When his ears pricked up, he was a dead ringer for Anubis in his full canine form. After he was killed on the road, he returned to me again and again as an impeccable guide, in dreams and visions.

Not long ago, noticing that Anubis was not on my desk, I went looking for him and found him in the cargo pocket of the shorts I was wearing on a hot day when I was leading an adventure in "Dreaming Like an Egyptian" at one of my favorite retreat centers. When I placed the little figure at my right hand, next to my computer keyboard, I noticed that he was missing part of his right leg. It had broken off just above the knee. I felt even more affection for the little figure, remembering a beloved childhood story of a one-legged toy soldier ("The Steadfast Tin Soldier"). I did not dwell for long on the symbolism of the damage to the right leg, around the knee.

That afternoon, I was lugging a heavy burden down the stairs in my home. Since suffering a knee injury six years before, I had taken stairs very carefully, usually holding on to the railing. But the awkward load I was carrying required both hands. At the top of the lower staircase, I had a sudden, vivid vision of myself falling down the stairs. I brushed this aside, not wanting to step into an anxiety projection.

I made it most of the way down the stairs, when I fell, landing heavily on elbows and knees. Blood gushed from my right arm, just below the elbow, but the worst damage was to my right knee. This was the knee that I injured before, when I severed one of the muscles in the quad that holds the kneecap in place. I managed to avoid surgery, but I have needed to be very careful on slopes and stairs, especially going down.

My knee creaked and complained and was soon swollen to twice its regular size. Several Aleve tablets and ice packs later, the swelling had subsided, and I could get around, limping a bit. I reflected on the fact that I was wearing the same polo shirt I was wearing on the day, six years before, when I first injured my right knee.

I went online in the evening and saw that a friend who has taken my dream-teacher training had fallen down stairs — on her face — about the same time.

I picked up my Anubis figurine and touched the broken leg. There really are things that like to happen together.

Limping around the lake in the park with my little dog the next day, I thought about lessons to be drawn. My fall down the stairs was eminently avoidable. I paid the price for failing to pay close attention to the kind of coincidence the ancients might have seen as a message from the realm of the gods, and then for confusing presentiment (my vision of the fall) with projection.

A jogger passed me on the path around the lake. On the back of her T-shirt was a spiral that formed a question mark. Another wink from the universe.

To walk the spiral path in life is to notice each time you come to a choice or a situation that resembles one you have encountered before, and then apply what you can learn from the past experience to avoid repeating mistakes. The secret logic of our lives is revealed through resemblances. Yet I failed to recognize and act on the message I might have received through the resemblance between Anubis' injury and my already wounded knee. I had experienced presentiment on many occasions and had learned that my body often reacts to events before the events take place. Yet I brushed aside my vision of the fall.

In the school of life, lessons are repeated until we graduate from each class.

The fall day was as crisp as a McIntosh apple just plucked from the tree. The sun was warm on my face, the breeze was cool in my hair, and my busted knee was working well enough to get me around the lake, though much more slowly than the runner with the spiral question mark. I resolved to be on the lookout for the next spiral question that might be put to me in life class.

◆

Looking for the spiral question involves much larger life issues than a knee injury. It means paying attention when you find yourself running into people and situations, choices and temptations, that remind you of a previous phase in your life.

In dreams, we often see a person or situation from our past before we find ourselves in contact in waking life with a new person or situation that resembles the old one. As the wheel turns in regular life, we find ourselves again at a familiar crossroads or in the presence of a new person who reminds us of someone we knew before.

Recognizing the similarity in either state of consciousness helps us ask the spiral question, which is essentially this: Do I want to repeat myself and go around again on the wheel of repetition or, learning from the past, am I ready to make wiser choices and go upward on the spiral of growth as I circle around?

GAME RULES FOR ASKING THE SPIRAL QUESTION

1. Notice when a life situation or an encounter with a new person strongly resembles a pattern or relationship in your past.
2. Recollect how things worked out before.
3. Harvest the lessons from that past situation and apply them, so that whether you choose to reenter a familiar situation or to step away from it, you are doing so with greater awareness of all that is involved.
4. Resolve to step off the wheel of repetition and follow the spiral path of personal growth, so that when things repeat, you handle them more wisely.

13. RECOGNIZE PERSONAL OMENS

Skepticism is the chastity of the intellect, according to Santayana. You should not give it up lightly, but you do not want to stay in a lockbox all your life.

I have a healthy skeptic in my left brain, and I want to keep him that way because he helps me test and verify things. But I sometimes ask him to stand aside when I want to enter into a new experience, in shamanic journeying, in the free play of creative imagination, or through encounters with sidewalk oracles and Kairos moments on the roads of life.

I am in favor of *practical* superstitions. The phrase sounds like an oxymoron, but it is worth recalling the original use of the word *superstition*. In ancient Rome, *superstitio* was a term applied to activities involving contact with the sacred that lay outside the official state religion. In Cicero's time, it was held to mean "fear of what stands above," but the earlier meaning involved "knowing what is hidden from others" in the manner of the seer or diviner. The association with ignorance, obfuscation, and old wives' tales comes later.

I am not in favor of the hand-me-down kind, inherited from Grandma or a tight community of old-time believers — unless they happen to work for you, as they sometimes do. When I speak of "practical superstitions," I mean personal omens, ones you can rely on because you have road tested them enough times. Here, I am offering a highly pragmatic approach to stuff that might seem absurdly loopy and impractical. This approach requires us to do some footwork and some self-checking, but this, too, is going to be fun.

You may notice that *some* old superstitions and nostrums work for you, maybe because one of those unseen hands that make things appear and disappear in the world around us chooses to work with your vocabulary of understanding. This is exactly what goes on in dreams and visions. Our dream producers, and greater powers, give us pictures and puns, dramas and deceptions, according to how we are able to perceive and receive.

So if I see a coin on the sidewalk, or in less convenient places — the floor by the cash register in the supermarket or between the boots of a TSA agent at an airport security check — I'll do everything possible to get it into my pocket. A rhyme out of boyhood will push me along:

> Find a penny, pick it up,
> then all day, you'll have good luck.

A humble penny is good, even if its features have been demolished by the hundred cars that have run over it, or it's green with age and weathering, or crusted with stuff I would rather not inspect too closely. A quarter is better, not only because values have changed since the penny rhyme started circulating, but because a quarter is the little offering I like to give to the Gatekeeper. Higher, as well as intermediary, denominations are quite acceptable.

Crows may have forty or more expressions, as my birdwatcher friends advise me, but I am tone deaf to most of them. However, I am capable of getting very specific signals from the number of crows (or of their larger cousins, the ravens) that appear in a certain moment. I am guided in this by another jingle from childhood:

> One for sorrow, two for joy,
> three for a letter, four for a boy

The "one for sorrow" is reinforced, for me, if a lone black bird flies in front of me, heading toward my left (the "sinister" direction). Since crows have become almost ubiquitous city dwellers, the simple count may be of little interest on an urban walk (one or two can suddenly become thirty or forty), but there are moments — especially in less populous areas — when you know that the number and behavior of the black birds are significant.

Getting more personal, a large and friendly black dog, especially when it appears under unlikely circumstances, is a good sign for me. This is no doubt largely because I shared my life in a critical period with two large and fiercely loyal black dogs who later appeared as impeccable guides in my dreams. There is a little edge of Anubis here, since, like ancient Egyptian children and dreamers, I have always loved the dog-man god who stands as Gatekeeper between the worlds and escorts traveling souls.

The red-tailed hawk is another of my personal omens — and far, far more. When I see a red-tailed hawk going my way, or enjoying a good roadkill dinner, I feel I have received a hearty thumbs-up (or rather, wings-up) for the day. I feel deep gratitude for all that Hawk has shown me — and shown to others through me — since I got in a car and drove 120 miles north of Manhattan in 1986. I was ready to change my life and was seeking the right ways. I thought they were likely to involve putting down deeper roots in my adopted country, living close to the land and its seasons.

On my very first weekend in what I learned to call "upstate" New York, I found a falling-down farmhouse with many acres. Half the land was virgin woodland that had never heard the sound of an ax. When I sat under an old white oak behind the house and watched a red fox trotting to or from his earth at the edge of a cornfield, I knew this was the right place. But in rational terms, a snap decision to move to this area, where I knew no one, too far to commute to the city, seemed nuts. I needed a confirming sign. As I leaned my back against the oak, a red-tailed hawk came circling overhead, squalling at me in a language I felt I would be able to understand if only I spoke hawk. She dropped a feather between my legs. It was the clincher; I bought the property.

When I have been uncertain of my way, or have simply needed further confirmation, Hawk has appeared on the roads of my life in quite literal ways. Once, when I was leading a fire cere-mony above a waterfall in the western Connecticut woods, a red-tailed hawk came circling overhead, dropping lower and lower, screaming at me like the one above the white oak at the farm. There was again the gift of hawk feathers, not from the bird itself but from a man who had come from Akwesasne, the Mohawk res-ervation on the Canadian border. He chose this moment to offer me hawk feathers as a gift from the descendants of an ancient Mohawk woman of power who called me, in dreams, after I moved to the farm.

There was a day when the black dog and the red-tailed hawk costarred in a synchronicity experience that is an amusing exam-ple of how practical superstitions *work*.

I was on the Connecticut shore, leading one of my trainings for teachers of Active Dreaming. We were very comfortably housed in a villa that had once belonged to Phil Donahue, the TV talk-show host, with wonderful views of Long Island Sound. After the close of our formal sessions that day, I was so engaged in lively conversation with my students that it slipped my mind that I had agreed with my hardworking book publicist that I would do a phone interview that afternoon with a California magazine she considered important.

When I remembered the phone date and looked at my watch, I saw I was over an hour late. I ran up to my room, hoping that I would be able to charm the magazine writer and pull off the inter-view. When I got her on the phone, her tone was icy. She had left me three messages. "I don't have time for this," she snapped. "I'm leaving the office."

I gave her honey enough for her to linger for a moment. She said, skeptically, "I might do the interview if you can explain this synchronicity stuff. I mean, how it works."

As she was speaking, I was standing on the balcony of my room in the TV star's former home, looking down at three fluffy bunnies nibbling the grass immediately below me. Very cute, Hallmark quality. As I watched, a red-tailed hawk dropped from the sky, talons outstretched. The hawk grabbed one of the bunny rabbits and rose straight up, a vertical takeoff-and-landing avian prodigy.

I wanted to describe this scene to the California writer as an example of how we can receive messages from the world. It was literally fresh meat. Then some instinct of caution came into play. The California magazine sounded oh so spiritually correct. The writer might be horrified by the idea that I would applaud the sighting of a hawk taking a bunny for dinner as a happy sign. Heck, she could be a vegan.

So I came up with an older story, one of many I have in my mental file of black-dog incidents. Before I was finished, I heard a dog barking on the California end of the line. "This is amazing," the writer said. "You are telling me a story about a black dog, and for the first time in my life, I have a black dog in my apartment. I'm dog-sitting for a friend."

She proceeded to interview me for the next hour, and the article she published was lovely. I knew this would turn out well. The hawk showed me, though I did not tell her that.

I pay attention to other personal omens that relate to roads far beyond the obvious. One of them is the appearance of a yellow Mini Cooper with a white roof. Whenever I see this zippy little car, in those exact colors, an inner alert goes off. It says: *Attention. Time Travel or Quantum Jumping in Progress.* I start looking around me for traces of a wrinkle in time or a reality shift between parallel event tracks.

Why a yellow Mini Cooper? Because I once dreamed of a reality break in which the Duke of Wellington, no less, came galloping out of a painting, swearing like a trooper, surrounded by his staff officers. This led into a thrilling action adventure in which contending teams were fighting for possession of the secret of time travel. The good guys — whose team my dream self joined — pursued the bad guys in a yellow Mini Cooper with a white roof.

The first time I narrated this dream (which has the makings of a movie script) was on a terrace outside a coffee shop in Seattle, over an Americano. At the precise moment when I began to describe the car used by the good guys, a yellow Mini Cooper identical to the one in the dream pulled into a parking spot right in front of us.

Personal omens work. If they don't, they are not practical, and you drop them from your list. A superstition is not practical if you just get spooked. Consider a cautionary tale from the life of a great writer.

Victor Hugo did not like the number thirteen, especially after what happened to him and his family in what he called the "Terrible Year," 1871. He left Paris on February 13 and found himself with thirteen people in a carriage on the train. When he got to Bordeaux, the address of the apartment where his son Charles and his daughter were lodged was 13, rue de la Corse. In the morning, the bill for the family breakfast at a restaurant was thirteen francs. Not long after, his son died, at age forty-four, of a massive heart attack.

So we might say that Hugo had reason for fear of the number thirteen, for which the scholarly name is "triskaidekaphobia." But the superstition later proved impractical, or at least to have an expiration date. When Hugo moved back to Paris, to a splendid apartment on the rue de Clichy in Paris (number 11) that became a famous address, the number of guests for dinner one evening was thirteen. This would not do. So a cab driver was invited to join the party. No doubt unused to all the rich food and drink, the cab driver spoiled the scene by throwing up copiously on an expensive carpet.

GAME RULES FOR
RECOGNIZING PERSONAL OMENS

1. Start by checking on superstitions you may have inherited or picked up from others. For example, that walking under a ladder or having a black cat walk in front of you is bad luck, or that having a bird poop on your head or your car might mean money is coming. Have any of these supposed omens worked for you the way they are supposed to? If so, keep them on your personal list of practical omens. If not, scratch them.

2. Check recurring images or incidents that catch your attention. Some people have strong feelings about numbers, both a repeated digit in one number (11:11, 2.22, etc.) and the recurrence of a certain number in many different places and situations in a certain time period.

3. Keep track of what happens after sightings of this kind. Does a certain kind of incident follow? Does the day turn out well or badly? Does the repeated number or similar sighting seem only to be saying, "Listen up, pay attention"?

4. Make a short list of your personal omens, the ones that seem to work, and pay attention to what follows your next sightings of them.

GAME #14. TRY THE
WHITE QUEEN GAMBIT

The body sometimes seems to "know" about a future event and responds as if that event had already taken place. An older term for this is *presentiment*. In the personal story I am about to tell, I think of it as *anticipatory symptoms*.

I went to my doctor's office for my annual physical. A new medical assistant took my blood pressure to get us started. Though she did not faint, my blood pressure was *much* higher than normal in the initial reading, much higher even than it had been when I had hobbled into that office two months before with a serious knee injury that had not yet been diagnosed.

I was startled by the blood pressure reading, since I was in excellent spirits and feeling no anxiety about this visit to the doctor.

"What do you want to do next?" the assistant asked. "The blood work or the EKG?"

"Let's go for the blood and get a little color." We briefly discussed how people react to having blood drawn. Personally, I have never minded the needle or the sight of the blood.

The assistant found the right place and stuck a needle in my left arm. As she extracted the needle after filling the syringe, she started a gusher. I had never seen anything like it in all my years of giving blood or blood specimens. In an instant, my whole left arm was covered in blood, and blood was spattered all over my freshly laundered linen pants.

The assistant squealed and rushed around trying to stop the blood flow at the same time as she attempted to treat my pants with hydrogen peroxide.

"You're upset!" she panted. The odd thing was that I really wasn't upset at all. I responded quite philosophically, as if the incident had taken place in the past, even as the blood was still spurting and spattering.

When things were under control, and she calmed down, I asked her to check my blood pressure again. "I want to test a hypothesis," I told her. "There's hard laboratory research that suggests that subjects can exhibit physical responses to events before the actual events take place. I want to check whether the spike in my blood pressure came about because — in some way — my body *knew* what was going to happen and had an anticipatory response."

She gaped at me, her eyebrows climbing her forehead, but she obliged.

She gasped when she gave me the new reading after releasing the pressure cuff. The first number had dropped by fifteen points; the second number had dropped by even more. She was amazed because she thought that after the crazy turmoil of the blood gusher, my readings should have gone up, not down.

"Not if my body knew and reacted to what was going to happen ahead of time," I suggested quietly.

When the doctor — a careful, conservative practitioner — came in and heard the data, he was quite impressed. "Maybe there's something in that theory," he allowed. He decided to check my blood pressure himself. The numbers dropped even lower.

To my mind, this is pretty persuasive firsthand evidence of the possibility that the body, through its own ways of knowing, may anticipate and respond to an event that has not yet taken place.

My favorite term for this kind of thing is the "White Queen Gambit." In *Through the Looking-Glass*, the White Queen screams *before* she pricks her finger. When her brooch pin subsequently flies open and she *does* prick her finger, she doesn't need to scream. "I've done all the screaming already," says the Queen. "What would be the good of having it all over again?"

It seems that the body, or the energy field around it, has intricate antennae that are constantly scanning for changes that will affect it. Most of us know about this from everyday experience. You have a "gut feeling" about something. You feel a sense of dread or elation, a lifting of the heart or a churning in the stomach, that has no evident explanation until a subsequent event takes place that would cause such physical reactions. When the event catches up with the anticipatory symptoms, you and your body may be quite calm and detached — because you've done the screaming or the hyperventilating already.

Scientific research into this phenomenon, which is sometimes described as "time-reversed interference," has been going on since the 1990s. Dean Radin ran tests at a University of Nevada lab in Las Vegas that involved showing subjects a series of photographs on a screen that were calculated to produce vividly contrasting somatic reactions, read by scanning heartbeat, perspiration, and so on. A photo of a peaceful rustic scene might be followed by hard porno or a picture of a gruesome crime scene. The very interesting finding was that many times subjects had the physical reactions a certain picture would be expected to produce, moments *before* the image came up on the screen.

I told the story of my gusher in the doctor's office to Larry Dossey, MD, one of the trailblazers for mind-body medicine in America, and asked him what he thought of my theory that the spike in my blood pressure was an anticipatory symptom. Dossey commented, "I think your interpretation is right on target. People need to know that these 'presentiment' effects are not just laboratory curiosities, but are phenomena that get played out in real life zillions of times, under our very noses, quietly, often without our realizing they're happening."

Maybe we can all do a little better if we let our bodies tell us what's going down. This is a case of "what the bleep we know" that we don't usually recognize that we know. I recommend learning to play the White Queen Gambit.

When I Did Not Want a Woman in My Lap

"Time for the rest of the novel," says the gate agent, after a pause in announcements. I thank him for starting my day right.

I take an aisle seat on the bulkhead on my first flight of the day. My in-flight reading is a crazy-funny novel by Douglas Adams called *Dirk Gently's Holistic Detective Agency*. The hero is a shabby, shifty student of coincidence who thinks that everything is connected and that he could solve a case by talking to a table leg if he was in the mood.

When I finish my coffee, I have nowhere to set down the cup, so I get up to put it in the trash in the galley. As I move, I sense a stir behind me. I turn to see a young woman starting to fall. She is crumpling slowly, like a figure in slow motion. Before anyone can catch her, she has fallen across the seat I have just vacated. She rolls until she is lying on the floor where my feet rested a moment ago.

The cabin crew is on this, asking over the intercom if there is a doctor or nurse on board. One of the flight attendants tells me, "Step over her, please."

I find an empty seat at the back of the plane and try to monitor the melee around the fallen woman. A flight attendant eventually tells me, "She's okay now. She just needed something to eat." All they had was pretzels and cheese crackers, but that was enough to get her back on her feet.

I return to my original seat and talk to the flight attendant. We agree that the timing was exquisite. The woman collapsed the moment I vacated my seat. "If you hadn't, she would have been in your lap."

"Feels like it means something, doesn't it? I'm not sure what that is. What would you think if this happened to you?"

The flight attendant is not sure. She glances at my battered copy of *Dirk Gently's Holistic Detective Agency*.

"Maybe you can find a holistic detective to figure it out for you."

"Funny. Usually I do that for myself."

What is the takeaway? Be ready for unexpected things to fall into my lap? Be sure to feed what needs to be fed?

My body knows the answer, but it takes my brain a while to produce the words. It was another case of presentiment. In my body, in my energy field, I knew, before she got to my row, that the hypoglycemic woman was going to fold over my place on the plane. An instinct of survival prompted me to move in the nick of time on the pretext of dumping a coffee cup.

GAME RULES FOR PLAYING
THE WHITE QUEEN GAMBIT

1. Pay attention to any sudden change in what you feel in your body.

2. Self-scan to check the source of the shift. If it does not seem to reflect the current state of your body or your feelings, ask whether it is possible that your body's sensors are picking up something that is happening at a distance, in space or time. You may be experiencing presentiment. Alternatively, you could be experiencing *telepathy*, which F. W. H. Myers, who invented the term, called "fellow-feeling at a distance."

3. Check for subsequent events or discoveries that may reflect that shift in your body.

4. Develop a personal code for signals of this kind. For example, you may find that a certain kind of sudden, sharp, and brief pain in the head is a message that someone is

trying to contact you. Or you may notice that when you smell a certain aroma that is not emanating from your immediate environment, it is a signal that someone at a distance who is connected to you has opened a link. Notice exactly how your body acts in anticipation of a subsequent physical event.

5. Log your findings in your journal.

GAME #15. PLAY THE
LIGHTENING GAME

Thirty people are sitting in a circle in front of a crackling fire under a stuffed moose head that has been up there for several generations. Outside, snow is falling on silver birches and pines. I have been gathering frequent fliers up on this mountain, on traditional Mohawk land in the Adirondack wilderness of New York, for many years. The mountain has a heart of red-garnet fire, and here the Deer energy is strong. Here we renew and deepen our bonds as a dreaming community, and this is a place where I love to test-fly new techniques.

The most important of all the techniques I first tested here is the one I decided to call Lightning Dreamwork. It is a fast, fun way for us to share dreams, receive helpful feedback, and encourage each other to take creative and healing *action* to embody the energy and guidance of dreams in everyday life. You can play this game just about anywhere, with just about anyone, unless they want to tell you what your dreams and your life mean. When we play this game, we are open to feedback from any viewpoint, but we do not tolerate people trying to play master, infallible psychic, or dream dictator. The dreamer is the final authority on the meaning of his or her dream. The role of others — whether or not they have certificates on their walls — is to help the dreamer become the author of meaning for her own dreams and her own life.

I called this simple four-step method for sharing dreams Lightning Dreamwork because it is meant to be fast, and to focus energy, like a bolt of lightning. I first demonstrated it to a general audience at the world conference of the Association for the Study of Dreams in New York in 2000. Since then, Lightning Dreamwork has become essential practice for Active Dreaming circles in more than twenty countries. You can find the rules in two of my previous books, *The Three "Only" Things* and *Active Dreaming*.

I invented the lightning method for dream sharing but noticed immediately that it can be used for almost any content, any story that needs to be told, with only minor adaptations of language.

I also noticed that very few people seem to be able to spell the word *lightning*. Again and again, in email and letters, in on-line forums and magazine articles, and even on websites and flyers promoting Active Dreaming workshops, it appeared as "lightening." Eventually, I tired of playing Spelling Instructor and instead applied the question, *What is showing through the slip?* If the *e* in *lightening* stood for *error*, it was an inspired mistake, the kind of mistake that inspires. It suggests that by playing this game, we may lighten up, spread a little light, and even practice enlightenment.

Beyond dream sharing, you can play the Lightening Game with just about any material — a vanity license plate you noticed in the street, a symptom, a family history, a call from your maiden aunt, the sound of the crows in the evergreens on a wintry morning shaking out their wings like straphangers folding and refolding newspapers. When it comes to offering feedback on the stories you hear, you will say, "If it were my life" or "If it were my experience" (rather than "If it were my dream"), when talking about something other than a dream.

GAME RULES FOR PLAYING THE LIGHTENING GAME

I. GET THE STORY (AND THE TITLE)

Your partner may be ready to share a dream, an oracle, or a life episode. Or you may take the initiative, saying, "Do you have a story?"

Everyone has a story. Sometimes people have been waiting half a lifetime for someone to ask. It is amazing what can pour out when we do that.

The trick now is to catch the story and let it assume the right shape.

We start by listening, by giving our full attention. We proceed by seeking, gently, to help the storyteller minimize clutter and self-blocking and say what they need to say as simply and clearly as possible. Do this, and you help your partner claim his or her voice and the power that comes when we learn to speak in a way that makes other people want to hear us.

Stories need titles. When you help someone tell a story, ask for a title.

2. Ask the Essential Questions

The first kind of question you want to ask is about *feelings*. How did you feel during this experience? How do you feel about it now?

The next type of question elicits a *reality check*. What do you recognize from this incident in the rest of your life? Has something like this happened before? Could something like this happen in the future? Does that person remind you of anyone else in your life? Do you have a habit of losing your keys? Do you get shivers when you see a fox?

Questions like these invite pattern recognition. You are building recognition that there are things that like to happen together. You are also exploring how a certain sign or symbol — in waking life or in dreams — may contain clues to coming events. What happened after you last saw a fox? If the time is always Now, that means that the future exists and is accessible in this present moment.

When you have heard the report of an oracle or incident, you may also want to ask, What do you want to know about this?

3. "If It Were My Life"

Now you can offer some feedback. A great way to start is by saying, "If it were my life" or "If it were my experience." When you are talking about a dream, of course you begin by saying, "If it were my dream." If you are commenting on a card that pops out of the oracle deck in the game you'll find in the next section, you will say, "If it were my card" or "If it were my oracle."

When you speak in this way, you are free to mention anything that comes to mind. You can bring in your own associations and bring up your own dreams and life memories. What comes to you from your own life in the presence of another person may be your very best way of understanding the other person's story.

You are free to say anything you like, as long as you say it nicely. That means owning your own projections and never presuming to tell another person what her experience means. It does not matter if what you say leaves that person absolutely cold. You don't need to come up with a correct interpretation. Your task is to guide the other person to finding what a certain experience means for him or her — and then to take appropriate action.

4. ACTION PLAN

Oracles and Kairos moments, like dreams, require action! The final step in the game is to ask: How are you going to honor this experience? Or: How are you going to act on the guidance you have received?

Creative action is always good: writing, drawing, making art or a performance from that special moment. Celebration may be the right action, or a personal ritual for giving thanks — or in certain cases, to propitiate the ancestors or other spirits you have neglected or offended.

A wild riff of unlikely and threatening events once led me to carry bread and wine to an ancient temple of the Great Goddess in Anatolia, returning gifts of the Goddess to the Goddess in reparation for a moment of folly that I realized had set those events in motion.

When we share our stories and our feedback, we can sometimes help each other come up with a one-liner, or "snapper," to carry some of the energy and guidance.

GAME #16. CONSULT THE INDEX CARD ORACLE

I invented an oracle game that is wonderful fun to play with a group. All you need is a set of old-fashioned three-by-five-inch index cards, enough pens or pencils to go around, and a shared readiness to play.

The game goes like this: You encourage everyone to call up a story from their life, or something with some story value. This might be a dream or a dream fragment. It might be something seen in the street. It might be a quote or a line from a song that is playing on that inner sound track right now.

You encourage everyone to write something from their material on one side of the index card. This text should be more than one word, but no more than will fit on one side.

Some people will need longer to write than others. You will be able to see who are the novelists or dissertation types and who are the reporters or short-story writers. When everyone has finished writing, you collect the cards and make them into a deck. You now have your oracle. For all its mundane materials, this could be the best divination deck you will ever encounter, because it is a onetime deck created just for this moment and will never be used in this way again.

The next step is to ask everybody who is playing to pose a question or a theme to the oracle. I like to get this clear and simple by having everyone fill in the blank in the following statement: "I would like guidance on _____." I urge all the players to pick a theme that has some real juice for them. You don't want to focus on more than one thing; that confuses the oracle. You should never try to be spiritually correct. If you want guidance on getting the money you need, or on your sex life, then say so.

Your theme could be quite finite: you could ask for guidance on the coming weekend, or a trip, or whether you should go to the dentist. Your theme could be huge, as in "I ask for guidance on my life direction." However you word your question, an oracle is always likely to speak to what you *need* to know, rather than what you *want* to know.

Get everyone to write down his or her theme, not on an index card, but preferably in a journal.

A volunteer will now play helper for the oracle and walk around the group with the deck. Players may pull a card at random or ask the helper to choose a card for them. "Hit me," is one way of asking for that, and it can produce interesting effects.

Either way, insist on this game rule: nobody will look at what is written on the card they have drawn until it is time. Every game requires rules, however silly they sound. You don't want to spoil the drama or blur the focus by having people sneak a peek at their cards too soon. In my workshops, I tell the group that if anyone is caught looking too soon, that person will be shamed, humiliated, and driven blubbering from the space. I confess that this inspires more laughs than terror. Almost every time, someone — usually the most respectable, responsible-seeming person in the group — will try to sneak a peek. It's almost irresistible.

Now we come to the heart of the game. The oracle is about to speak.

Choose who will be the first person to hear from the oracle. In the workshops, I spin a drumstick to pick that person. However you pick in your group, the first person to read their card is going to set the model for the others. So let's get this right.

Ask the person who is going first to state their intention: "I would like guidance on _____." Assure them that they are now going to receive a direct response to that theme from the oracle, through the words written on the card. The text may be mysterious or ambiguous; this is how oracles stay in business long-term. The writing may be hard to decipher. It may be necessary to turn to the author or someone else in the group for help with translating. This will be part of the message, possibly indicating that help is needed with this issue and that help is available (or not, depending on how this turns out).

The oracle will now speak.

In the workshops, we sometimes build up the drama shamelessly at this point, with a few drumbeats and some foot stomping and clapping. This is great stuff in a party version, at home or wherever you get together with friends. It's showtime!

The seeker reads the text on the card aloud, in front of the group. It may be necessary to read more than once, to figure out the words and then to start to absorb the meaning.

The message may be quite direct. It may contain specific details that speak to the seeker's current situation very precisely. It will of course be synchronistic. Someone who had recently lost a dog received a card written by another person in the group who had lost a dog, referring to a dream in which that beloved companion returned as a guide. Someone who is passionate about cultivating lilies received a card that was inspired by Georgia O'Keeffe's paintings of calla lilies.

Linking the card to the seeker's theme may require similar detective skills, and the same "talent for resemblances," that are needed for linking a dream to a prior intention. Here you can have others in the group contribute. You want to say, "If it were my card," or "If it were my theme," or "If it were my life," and then you can say whatever comes to you.

Solitaire Version of the Index Card Oracle

The coincidence card game is best fun when played in a group of six or more. However, there is a solitaire version, actually a couple of them.

The more solitary of these versions requires you to start making your private deck by writing down daily one-liners, dream summaries, and quotes that catch your attention on one side of a set of index cards. You'll need to allow time for the deck to grow so that you won't just be seeing familiar messages. Put the cards in a box. Let the deck grow for at least a few months, and then you'll be ready to surprise yourself by pulling a card at random and seeing how a message you gathered some time ago may speak of your situation now.

If you play the card game fairly regularly with others, you can make a solitaire deck from the cards you pulled from others. This is likely to be a wilder deck. I have many decks of this kind, with words written in many hands and several languages. I can no longer remember who wrote most of the cards, or where we played the game, or what intention I had set in consulting the card oracle for myself. So there is a real sense of mystery, mingled with familiarity, when I draw from my solitaire deck, the mix of feelings that come when you are on the edge of a Kairos moment.

I am doing this now. I open a little black chest with a miniature Excalibur sword on the side. It's a cigar box; the cigars once in it were forgettable, but I love the box. I let my hand find the right card in the right index card deck among the four that are inside. I look at the handwriting. I do not recognize it, but it is legible and distinctive. The *F*'s have high loops; they look like feathers, like plumes. The *I* is quite unusual. The stem is either flying forward, making the shape of an arrowhead, or bending back, to make the shape of talking lips. The text, written from top to bottom rather than across the card, gives me this: "The fox was bleeding from his throat which was later healed. I walked into the healing sea confused, directionless, and emerged whole and independent. A family of owls assisted me in his 'becoming.'"

I read this and breathe the words *Thank you*. My first writing of the day was about the fox, specifically about an oracle associated with fox spirits in Japan. But words were not yet flowing freely, and I felt uneasy and confused about how to structure drafts and materials I had been assembling. The card confirmed for me that I was on the right track and would have all the guidance and help I would need. The owl is a wise bird and the companion of a wise goddess who has helped me before; I once climbed to the ruins of her mountain temple at Priene in Anatolia to return thanks.

Now I decide to reach into another of my solitaire decks, one composed in the solitary way of accumulating little stories and snappers and dream summaries in one's own time. I read this, in my own hand, which is even legible here: "Great News: a train of crystallized pineapple has been sighted, and it's coming your way."

I smile, remembering that I dreamed this just before the media announced that a torrential rainstorm beating down on California had been named the Pineapple Express, since it started in Hawaii (where I would be traveling in a couple of months). The happy energy of the dream was more important than the precognitive elements. I drew a childlike picture of a pineapple train and colored it in blazing yellows. With the card in my hand, I feel infused by the same joyful energy. Sometimes the greatest gift of these games is simply a shot of juice.

GAME #17. WRITE A MESSAGE WITHOUT SENDING IT

The next game is an exercise in telepathy inspired by a game invented and played by Mark Twain, who was a keen student of coincidence.

He wrote an article about the game, titled "Mental Telegraphy," but waited for more than a decade to publish it, fearing ridicule or incredulity. When public interest and scientific research (notably, the investigations of the young Society for Psychical Research in England) began to catch up with his own findings, he came out with the article in *Harper's* magazine.

He chronicles many examples of the phenomenon of "crossed letters." You know the kind of thing: you write to someone (or just think about them) — maybe someone you have not been in contact with for months — and then you get a letter or a call from them the same day or very soon after.

There are a couple of things at play here — well evidenced by Twain's personal anecdotes. The first is the reality of distant communication between minds keyed to similar wavelengths. Twain's most amazing example is the Great Bonanza book. One afternoon, as he tells it, Twain was seized with the passionate conviction that a great book could be written about the silver bonanza in Nevada. His old newspaper colleague Wright would be the man to do it, but Twain was so possessed by the idea that he immediately roughed out an outline and sample chapters to get his old friend started.

He was preparing to mail all this material to Wright when he received a package in the mail. Before opening the package, Twain told the people with him that he was going to deliver a "prophecy"; he declared that the package contained a letter from his old friend Wright, with his drafts for a book on the Great Bonanza. And so it did. This incident convinced Twain not only that mental telegraphy is real, but that it can be strong enough to transport the complete content of a book across three thousand miles. Fortunately, Twain and Wright were good friends, and Twain had already determined that the Great Bonanza book was to be done by Wright; otherwise, the mental transfer (from Wright to Twain) could have resulted in two books and charges of plagiarism.

Minds resonate with each other, and in doing this, transfer ideas and messages back and forth. We can move to pluck the strings as well as wait for them to vibrate. A case in point — from Twain's account — involves an American on the Grand Tour in Europe who was desperate since he had received no news from his son, back in San Francisco, in many months, despite sending several letters. Twain urged him to send a cable, which might sound like the merest common sense. Here's the uncommon sense: Twain further told the worried father that it did not matter where he sent the cable. "Send it to Peking, if you like." All that mattered was that he should take the step of sending a cable. If he did that, Twain promised, he would have news from his son. The father sent the cable, and the next day received a letter from his son explaining that he had left San Francisco months before on a slow boat and was now acting on his first opportunity to mail a letter. The cable did not prompt the letter, which was mailed long before; but the two communications coincided, just as Twain had promised.

My friend Wanda Burch had an experience resembling that of the father Twain pushed to send a cable anywhere at all. Wanda had been waiting for many months to see whether a publisher to whom she had sent the manuscript of her first book was willing to publish it. I urged her to contact an agent. I suggested one agent by name, but also told her, "You can contact any agent at all. Just get in touch." She objected that she liked the publisher (to whom I had introduced her) and, being a patient person, was willing to wait. "If you want to hear from the publisher," I told her firmly, "you have to talk to the agent. This is not about getting an agent to push through a deal. It's about sending out a certain kind of signal, about plucking strings of possibility." Still reluctant, Wanda contacted an agent. Immediately, the publisher contacted her, offering an advance for her book. These two communications were unconnected in any mechanical way. Indeed, when Wanda heard back from the agent two weeks later, she was able to tell her that she no longer needed an agent because she had negotiated her own deal, no mean feat for a first-time author.

Mark Twain developed what he liked to call a "superstition" about this. He decided that if he wanted to hear from someone, he would write that person a letter and then tear that letter up. Infallibly, he claimed, he would then receive a letter from the person to whom he had written.

This is an interesting line of experiment. Few of us send real letters by mail anymore, so it might be appropriate to try doing it by email, text, or Facebook message. Here's how to play:

GAME RULES FOR MENTAL TEXTING

1. Compose an email, text, or other message to someone you would like to hear from.
2. Do not send the message. Save it in the appropriate format, in a drafts folder or as a Word document.
3. Wait to see if your target contacts you of his or her own volition.

Probably the best target to use for this game is someone with whom you have had contact but do not know well, or with whom you have not had contact for some time. You could try writing to a complete stranger, of course, and see whether this brings any results.

When Writing the Letter Is Enough

I have often recommended writing a letter without sending it, as a means of expressing love and forgiveness or sending blessing when ordinary channels of communication are difficult or unavailable. I have advised people to write to deceased family members and friends. Most important, I have counseled people who need to seek healing and clearing with a living person to use this method when ordinary communication has broken down. The unsent letter becomes a powerful vehicle for the wishes that need to be transmitted. Beyond simple meditation or "wishcraft," this method can effect extraordinary positive changes both in the recipient and the sender.

CHAPTER FIVE

ON OTHER PLANES

Some people pursue enlightenment by sitting quietly and probing
their inner consciousness. I make plane reservations.

— MADELEINE ALBRIGHT, *Prague Winter*

airos moments multiply when we are in motion. I spend half
my days traveling across the world map to lead workshops.
This involves spending a great deal of time at airports and on airplanes, and plenty of experience of having to change plans and
change itineraries because of missed connections, flight delays,
and other hazards of the sky roads. You don't need to tell me
about sore knees, or the fellow who throws his seat back into your
lap, or sneezers who don't cover their noses, or airline food. What
keeps me cheerful even on the longest journeys is the way that
chance comes into play and rarely fails to provide a fresh story. I
will put up with almost anything if it has story value.

You may have noticed that when plans go awry, the Trickster comes into play. In *The Three "Only" Things*, I introduced
the theme of synchronicity with five stories of chance encounters that were mediated by missed connections or canceled flights.
The stories in this chapter are fresh, from other encounters on

other planes. In some of them, it is difficult not to feel the presence of spirits — jesting, confirming, or importunate — beyond the human personalities engaged in conversation.

SPILLED COFFEE EN ROUTE
TO MONTANA

When I boarded my first flight of the day to Bozeman, Montana, I was alerted to the possibility that there might be some mishap ahead. The fellow who took his seat across the aisle from me turned to me, staring, and announced, "This will be an eventful flight." I didn't ask him what he meant, but I got the message that there might be a surprise in store of the less-than-welcome kind.

As soon as we were in the air, the fellow sitting in front of me threw his seat back so he was virtually in my lap, so I could not bring my table down properly. I realized I'd better be careful with the coffee I was about to order from the flight attendants, especially since they were quite distracted, caught up in intense gossip of their own; they were mixing up orders and had already spilled someone's ice. I nursed my coffee carefully, when it came, and got it down safely. Nonetheless, I continued to feel some anxiety, edged with irritation.

Then the woman to my left spilled her coffee all over my left leg. As she gasped apologies, I sloshed water from a bottle over the vast and spreading stain, grateful that I was wearing jeans instead of the linen pants I had considered earlier that morning.

I turned to my rowmate and said, "Since you have introduced yourself by spilling coffee over me, I need you to explain yourself. There is clearly some reason we are meant to have a conversation." Yes, I talk to strangers like this, all the time.

For the rest of the flight, she explained her family, her work as a special-ed teacher, her hopes for retirement, and why she was traveling with her husband to Milwaukee (to visit a married daughter who was a product manager for a department store chain). Then she started telling me about Bozeman, Montana.

"Wait a minute," I interrupted. "You told me earlier you've never been to Bozeman, and you're not going there today. How do you know about it?" She told me that, last thing the night before, she watched an episode of *House Hunters* on TV in which a couple were checking out real estate options and lifestyles in Bozeman. Through coincidence, she was prepped, to a small extent, to tell me something about a town I was visiting for the first time.

This was mildly entertaining, but no big deal. As I waited for my connecting flight at O'Hare airport, I reflected that the main interest of my travel experience thus far might be that it suggested the workings of presentiment, when we feel or sense something before it occurs. I seemed to know that coffee was going to be spilled. When the spill took place, my prior anxiety and irritation evaporated. I did not need to express them now that the incident they foreshadowed had taken place, as the White Queen in *Through the Looking-Glass* did not need to scream after she pricked her finger, since she had screamed in advance.

I was curious to see what "objective chance" might bring me on my second and longer flight. I found myself immediately engrossed in a wonderful conversation with my new rowmate. When I mentioned I was speaking at a bookstore in Bozeman that evening (a marvelous independent called the Country Bookshelf), she immediately offered to put me in touch with another fine independent bookstore in the town where she lives.

When she told me she had been a pediatric nurse for more than twenty years, the conversation deepened. I told her that over that same period, nurses have been the number one occupational group represented in my workshops. Nurses have immediate uses for the techniques of shamanic dreaming and are called on to play the role of spiritual guides, and sometimes psychopomps on the roads through death. We discussed specific techniques that can help nurses to play these roles and to hold their own in the presence of doctors who act as if *MD* means "minor deity."

Our talk ranged wide and deep — from her vivid account of riding in a hay cart among a herd of bison during a thunderstorm on a ranch in Wyoming, to the life of the Lakota at Pine Ridge and the visions of Black Elk, to the work of an archaeoastronomer who discovered that an ancient arrangement of stones in Chaco Canyon casts the shadow of a great bear at the equinox.

Then came the climactic exchange. I was not surprised to learn that my neighbor was a writer, given her great literacy and narrative skill. What was she working on now? "A memoir of my life when I was three years old," she told me. She explained that she felt that this year in her early life was shadowed by a coming death; her father died when she turned four.

I felt shivers running through my energy field. Because, for the previous three days, I had been writing a sketch of my life when I was three years old, a time in my early boyhood that was also shadowed by death. I died for the first time, in my present life, at age three, losing vital signs in a hospital in Hobart, Tasmania, after I contracted pneumonia. One of the doctors told my parents that I "died and came back." That event changed everything.

So here we were, on the plane to Bozeman: two people who had just discovered that each had been called to write a memoir of what happened at age three, in a time when a coming death — my own temporary death and her father's permanent one — cast a shadow before it. I was grateful for a nod from the universe toward my efforts to write the book that was later published as *The Boy Who Died and Came Back*. I also felt I had been rewarded for keeping my sense of humor through the spilled-coffee incident. *Don't leave home without your sense of humor.* That trumps all the other rules of life mentioned in this book.

FLYING WITH A
DREAM OF SHIVA'S BULL

The previous chapter described the practice of walking with a dream. This is a story of flying with a dream. As so often is the case, it reflects how dreams coach us for coming events and how we may not be able to grasp the relevance and full significance of a dream until a waking event catches up with it.

On April 17, 2014, I recorded this dream:

> I am on the lawns of a center or temple near a large sculpture of a sacred animal, a giant bull. In the dream, I have a statuette of a bull that matches the giant version. I carefully draw a thick black line on the miniature figure, from between the horns along the ridge of the back. When I am finished, I place the statuette on the plinth where the giant bull stands. I am satisfied I have made the correct offering.

I woke from this dream tremendously excited, but mystified about what exactly was going on. The dream location reminded me of a yoga center where I used to teach and had powerful visions of Shiva. I suspected that the bull statues were of Nandi, the bull of Shiva.

The match between the miniature and giant statues reminded me of another Hindu-themed epiphany in my travel chronicles. Seven years earlier, returning from an emergency trip to London that had interrupted a book tour, I took an airport shuttle from O'Hare to the northern suburbs of Chicago. I noticed that the Indian driver had a huge crystal figure of Ganesa on his dashboard. I pulled out a miniature crystal Ganesa from my pocket. A friend had pressed this on me just before my trip. The two Ganesas matched perfectly. I showed my little Ganesa to the shuttle driver, who beamed and exclaimed, "You know Ganesa! Your doors will be open!" I took this double manifestation of the Remover of Obstacles as an excellent portent for the rest of my book tour, and so it proved to be.

A week after my dream of the bulls, I boarded a plane for Paris, en route to teaching in southern France. My rowmate was a lively, intelligent woman from India. When we struck up a conversation, she told me she was making an emergency trip home to Bangalore because her mother had been diagnosed with a life-threatening illness. Our talk went deep. We talked for hours about death, and imagery for healing, and many elements in Hindu religious beliefs and practices. I spoke of my experiences of Yama, the Hindu death lord, and Ganesa, the opener of doors. Then I said, "Nandi."

My rowmate smiled with her whole being. She told me there is a temple of Nandi in her home city, Bangalore, with a giant bull statue carved from granite. She added that she keeps a miniature statue of Nandi close and regards him as another important protector and gatekeeper. We discussed some specific pujas (offerings) her family might now make to call on the greater powers according to their traditions. The woman from Bangalore said, "Are you sure you weren't born in India? I feel you are here tonight to remind me of some of the deepest beliefs and practices of my own tradition about how to approach death and the sacred." She volunteered to send me a miniature figure of Shiva's bull.

DEATH RHYMES ON THE WAY TO MADISON

I am catching an early flight on Thursday to keep my date as Death in Madison, Wisconsin, where I am leading a weekend workshop titled "Making Death Your Ally." I pause for a cup of coffee at the café near the A gates at my local airport. The old guy behind the counter has been working there forever, and always seemed happy to see me. But today he freezes before greeting me. "They're calling my dad," he explains, referring to an airport announcement I missed. "Steven Noble. That's my dad's name. Of course, he's dead."

"Maybe your dad is being called to a better place," I suggest as he works the coffee urn.

The announcement is repeated. "Passenger Steven Noble, please return to the security check."

"Or maybe your dad left something behind," I amend my suggestion.

"Maybe what he left behind was *me*," says the guy behind the counter, thoughtfully, as he hands me my coffee.

On the first leg of my trip, I open a selection of William James' writings, acquired the day before, to an introductory chapter titled "A Conversational Encounter with William James." The young woman in the seat next to me gapes at the page, wide-eyed.

"That's my dad's name," she tells me. "William James." Another rhyming theme for the day is asserting itself; the first two people I encounter on the road recognize their fathers' names.

Changing planes at O'Hare airport, I go to use a restroom on the F concourse. The scene inside the men's room is rather strange. Men are standing about motionless, all watching the maneuvers of a maintenance man who is down on the floor on his back, wriggling his large body so as to get his head and torso under the locked door of a stall. He sputters with shock or disgust as he gets far enough to unlock the door from the inside. Another janitor moves to block our view of whatever is inside the stall. After a muffled conference, one of them takes off in a hurry, pulling out a walkie-talkie. "Is there a problem?" I ask as he hurries by. "No problem," he responds, with a trace of dry humor. I don't need to ask anything more, because I get it. Death stopped by that restroom just before I did.

Now I'm on my second flight of the day, on the little puddle-jumper that will take me from Chicago to Madison. There's a holdup. An airline staffer with a manifest explains, "We have an extra body on board." It seems there is one more passenger on the plane than is identified on her chart. She goes through the plane row by row, asking all of us for our names and our boarding passes. I notice that the woman across the aisle from me is reading a mystery novel with a bookmark that says "Booked for Murder."

The man next to me gives his name, when asked, as "Flatland." I turn to him and observe, "That's an unusual name." He explains that his family took the name from the district in Norway from which they emigrated. I tell him about the parable of Flatland devised by Edwin Abbott Abbott to help us imagine what it would be like to see and operate from the fifth dimension instead of merely the 3-D reality (plus time) we ordinarily inhabit. Abbott's Flatland is a 2-D world in which everything is completely exposed to a citizen of 3-D reality who can materialize and dematerialize and move things around in a godlike (or ET) fashion incomprehensible to inhabitants of the horizontal universe.

In the midst of this conversation, the mystery of the extra body is resolved. An infant has been assigned a seat in the manifest, though not a boarding pass. We are airborne, soon looking down on the dairy farms of Wisconsin cheese country.

At Madison's Dane County airport, Karen McKean, my friend who is coordinating my Death workshop for me, is waiting next to a display case that features a curious composite sculpture: a skeletal figure with a Death's head at its center.

Death has not finished rhyming. When I arrive at the CBS studios for an interview with *Live at Five*, I am given coffee in a black mug with the logo of a (Winnipeg) taxidermy company, "a family tradition." When I go on from the interview to have

drinks with a friend before a bookstore event, she tells me she just
dreamed her husband died from a heart attack.

FLYING WITH THE
DEATH'S HEAD DOMINATRIX

We draw people and events toward us according to our ruling
interests and passions. I have felt a close engagement with Death
all of my life, starting with three near-death experiences in childhood. I lead workshops in which I help people to encounter Death
as an ally rather than as a formless dread or a grim reaper. I started
writing a tale about a writer who makes a deal with Death. All
the same, I was not prepared for the Death's head dominatrix to
appear on a plane two days later.

I notice her coming down the aisle of the plane, towering
above her male companion and other passengers in her high-
heeled black boots, her narrow form made still taller by a black
silk top hat. I stand up for her when she indicates that she is going
to take the seat next to mine. Her companion takes the window
seat. As they settle, I notice her gloves. They have Death's heads
on the backs. Still wearing the top hat, she might have stepped out
of the scene in *The Master and Margarita* where Mephistopheles
and his talking cat put on a sinister magic show in Moscow.

I tell her, "You look like a magician."

"Retired magician," says her companion.

"So what does a retired magician do?" I ask a bit later.

She considers this for a moment before she replies, with a
faint Southern drawl, "Let me say that spankings are my friends."

Oh, uh…I am talking with a dominatrix. It is entirely obvious when I take a closer look at her outfit, black leather over
a black-lace bustier, and those high, high boots. I am not sure I
want to pursue conversation. I open the book I have brought for
in-flight reading. It is Peter Kingsley's *A Story Waiting to Pierce*

You. Then I catch the rhyme. I chuckle at the thought of how Peter might twitch if he realized that someone hearing the title of his book about ancient shamans might think it was a prospectus for whatever services my neighbor offers her clients.

The dominatrix cranes around, inspecting the rest of the economy cabin. "I have a good feeling about this flight," she announces. "Every seat is taken. When a plane is going to crash, on average 20 percent of the seats are vacant because people sense something wrong and don't show up at the airport. There was a special on the Discovery Channel about this."

"Very interesting."

I put my nose back in *A Story Waiting to Pierce You* until after takeoff, when she starts talking about crows and ravens. She watches them very closely. She says she knows a big raven with a large harem. I point out that this would be rare indeed, since ravens generally live in couples and — like many other birds — mate for life.

She wants to tell me about a place she knows where crows are sometimes so thick on the ground that they cover a whole field. "I've seen one crow talking while all the others are listening. I think of that one crow as the storyteller. When the crow speaker is done, sometimes all the crows take off at once. But sometimes they fall on the crow speaker and peck him to death. What do you think of that?"

Before I come up with a response, she adds, "Native Americans say that when the other crows kill the speaker, it's because he is a bad storyteller."

Now this is a story that pierces me. Over the previous week, at my writing retreat in the foothills of the Cascades, I created a "frame" story within which I could write other stories. In the frame story, inspired by another recent plane trip, the narrator is riding with Death in the darkened cabin of an airplane. Death reminds him that they have an arrangement: he must keep coming up with stories that entertain Death, or else his life will be over. Now the Death's head dominatrix is telling me about how a murder of crows deals with a storyteller who fails to entertain.

The conversation gusts and pauses and picks up again. Each time, she is the one to break silence. She says, out of nowhere, "Do you believe that dreams show us what happens after death?"

"Absolutely. In dreams, we receive visitations from the dead, and we travel to places where they live. I have written books about this."

"My first husband was shot to death at breakfast time in a diner, with a cup of Americano in his hand, by a crazy guy who was looking to kill someone else. I grieved so deep I thought I would join him. Then I had a dream that was more than a dream. I sat up in bed in the middle of the night, and he was there. He looked good. He wanted to tell me what he is doing where he now lives. He was a musician. He told me that now he works up music and special effects for dreams that are being produced for people who are sleeping."

This is fascinating. I tell her I think it is entirely possible that crews like this engage in dream production. "There are many kinds of dreams, and some feel like productions custom made for the dreamer. I have always been curious about who is in the film crews." This would be a pretty good job for a dead musician.

After another pause, the dominatrix starts playing literary adviser. She has story ideas for me. They come from her uninvited, blown on a strange wind. "I would love to read the story of Jezebel, told from her point of view," she announces. "I am fascinated by the Phoenicians. Their witches were very good with dreams."

I am speechless, a rare condition for me. One of the stories I was writing for Death in my writing retreat is about a Roman centurion whose mistress is a Phoenician witch who talks to him about dreams. Is the dominatrix scooping impressions out of my energy field? Is her dead husband whispering in her ear?

"I wasn't really a magician," she says as the plane descends. "I worked for a circus as an aerialista. But I did magic, especially on that massage table I had going at the same time." She plays with a long braid that escapes the top hat, and comes back to the spankings. "How do you tell a stranger you're a dominatrix?" she muses.

"When and how did you recognize your calling?"

"Growing up in the Deep South with Jehovah's Witness parents helped. Then people kind of got me typed when we played cops and robbers as kids, and I always wanted to be the cop with the handcuffs."

I thought about her dead husband's account of doing special effects for the producers of dreams. I wondered whether a film crew of that kind was stage-managing this whole encounter.

The companion of the dominatrix had dozed throughout the flight. As we land, he gets up groggily, and she introduces him as "Homer."

"Good luck on your odyssey, Homer," I quip, my spirits rising now that we are back on the ground.

"All I want to do is build a bowling alley," says Homer, inexplicably. "A one-lane bowling alley. Something to do when I get old."

Whoever is scripting all this has a very strange sense of humor. I trust it is a good enough story to entertain Death.

THE HARUSPEX FLIGHT

I am not always overjoyed to be upgraded to first class on airplanes, because the stories I hear are usually better in coach. But on my way home from a very short trip to England for the funeral of a friend, I was delighted to be promoted to the front cabin, expecting nothing more than extra legroom, free drinks, and edible food. My rewards proved to be greater than these.

The pleasant woman who took the seat next to me spoke in a soft Southern accent. When she told me she was from Mississippi, I could not resist telling her that within the past week, I had recorded a dream in which I was making my way to Grant, Mississippi. I noted that "Grant" seemed an unlikely name for a place in Mississippi, given its history with General Ulysses S. Grant in the Civil War. "Oh, I don't know," she responded. "My daughter would like a grant for her research."

She explained that her daughter was majoring in Latin at the University of Mississippi and was also keenly interested in archaeology and the religions of the ancient world. "She just wrote a paper on Etruscan divination that her professor thinks is wonderful. There was a special class of Etruscan priests who got messages by looking at the livers of animals. There's a term for that, which I forget."

"*Haruspicy*," I suggested.

"That's it!" My neighbor's eyes widened a little. "What are the odds of meeting a stranger on a plane who would know about that?"

I started rattling off a few things I had learned about methods of divination in the ancient world. Haruspicy — also called *hepatoscopy* or *hepatomancy* — was the inspection of the liver of sacrificed animals. *Extispicy* was a broader term for examining the entrails, especially the intestines. *Scapulomancy* was the study of the shoulder blade of a slain animal. All these methods, probably first developed in early Mesopotamia, were regarded as critical in making major decisions. Babylonian kings and generals went to war with a *baru* priest in their entourage, ready to kill a sheep to check from the folds and color of the liver which side the gods

were on. The supposedly rational Athenians behaved the same
way. The Hittites looked at animal livers to get a second opinion
on the meaning of royal dreams.

I noted that my first job was as a junior professor of ancient
history at the Australian National University and that I had written on ancient divination. Since first reading about the history of
Rome, I had been fascinated by the special role of the Etruscan
priestly caste, under both the republic and the empire, in decisions of state. As I understood these things, the haruspex (literally
"the reader of the victim") who examined livers was consulted
on matters of high policy, such as war and peace, and was always
an Etruscan. An interesting paradox — that Romans turned to
an order of divination priests drawn from a people they had conquered.

"Oh, you have to talk to Juliana," my neighbor said. "I'll
swap seats with her after lunch." It seemed that her two daughters, who had gone with her to London for a week of theatergo-
ing, were back in coach.

After the meal, the switch was made. Juliana proved to be a
brilliant student with a searching mind, who introduced me to
sources and aspects of the subject that were previously unknown
to me. She had recently attended a seminar with Jean MacIntosh
Turfa, the author of a scholarly book titled *Divining the Etruscan
World: The Brontoscopic Calendar and Religious Practice*. It was
my turn to receive an unusual word under unlikely circumstances.
Brontoscopic refers to a method of divination by listening to the
sound of thunder. The Etruscans kept a calendar that linked thunder and lightning to outbreaks of disease and social events, day
by day, through a lunar year. The *fulgurator* was a specialist in
divination by thunder and lightning.

I was soon scribbling notes. My new rowmate was very
knowledgeable about Near Eastern parallels and precedents for

the Etruscan diviners consulted by the Romans. She described an Etruscan bronze mirror that shows a haruspex with one foot on a rock and wings on his back as he inspects a liver, clearly depicted as a link between the worlds of men and gods. She compared models of livers, made in clay by the Babylonians and in bronze by the Etruscans, used to guide the diviner on what to look for in a liver. An Etruscan model, intricately divided by many criss-crossing lines, appears to have the name of a deity inscribed in each section.

My young mentor had fascinating views on why the liver was regarded as so important for people wishing to know what was going on and whether the deities were on their side. A sacrificial animal may have been exposed to similar ailments and parasites as humans in the same environment and may have consumed some of the same foodstuffs.

The liver was understood to be a vital organ, not least for its role in cleansing the blood. It was seen as a seat of emotions and even of the soul.

We laughed over Cicero's comments about divination by animal innards. The Etruscans, he noted, were "raving mad about entrails." Yet while his equestrian nose twitched over superstitious mumbo jumbo, Cicero allowed that since "the gods are real," they may choose to make their wishes known even through the state of a slaughtered animal's entrails. He spoke of the *etrusca disciplina* — the name the Romans gave to Etruscan divination — with respect and narrated the myth of its founder, Tages, in his essay *On Divination*. Well might Cicero treat the craft of the haruspex with caution and respect. It was a haruspex, Vestrinius Spurinna, who delivered the famous warning to Julius Caesar to beware the ides of March.

I have a fresh list of reading and research assignments that I will happily pursue, though maybe at a comfortable remove from future mealtimes. I see that the best liver for haruspicy was one that had just been carved from the animal victim, still warm and quivering in the diviner's hand. As I embark on fresh research, I find that the Hittites also liked to observe the spasms of the dying animal as its organs were removed. I won't be eating liver, with or without onions, anytime soon.

At the time of this encounter, I was revisiting ancient sources on divination as part of my research for this book. We again see how chance encounters may be guided or generated by our interests and studies. I considered expanding the menu for this book to include an account of ancient methods of divination, including haruspicy, but decided that animal sacrifice did not need to be placed on the menu of sidewalk oracles in today's world.

BETTER TO BLOW UP ON THE GROUND THAN IN THE AIR

The four-hour wait at Newark airport for the second leg of my flight to Istanbul, the long one, was not so bad. The educated, quietly humorous man from Galway on the seat next to me at the airport bar had a fine way with words. He described someone who gave fake smiles as "looking like he had a coat hanger stuck in his mouth."

We boarded the 767 on time, and I was delighted to find that I had more legroom in Economy Plus than I had ever enjoyed on a plane, even in first class. I helped the woman who took the seat next to me with her bag, and commented on our luck. But her mind was somewhere else. She started complaining that she could not see the screen where she could watch her personal choice of movies, and this was not okay. "I paid for this seat," she snapped at an airline person, "and I can't get through the flight without movies."

She calmed a little when she was shown how to extract the

screen that had been fitted into the arm of her seat. It seemed that our legroom was due to the fact that we were seated in what was once an exit row. The exit was gone, but not the other features — no fold-down table, but all that space.

I could not resist teasing my rowmate a little over losing her cool when in fact the world and those around her were treating her notably well. She spoke of the stress she'd been under. I gently observed that the universe responds to the attitudes we project, so we want to check those attitudes and choose where we put our energy. I said, "This is one of the things I help people to see." She turned a bit chilly, but a few minutes later, she asked me to explain what I do. I told her, "I help people to be choosers in life." She allowed that she basically agreed with what I had said about choosing our attitudes; she practiced meditation and had studied with Zen teachers and others.

"Our personal truth," I said, "is what we remember and act upon."

She readily agreed. She was now eager to talk about everything, from our favorite books, to how she could improve her dream recall, to methods of conflict resolution, about which she proved to be highly knowledgeable. I started to look forward to an interesting conversation.

Our big plane taxied down the runway. Then there was a pop like the cork coming out of a bottle of champagne, except that this was no cause for celebration. The lights went out, the AC died, and the plane came to a total and silent stop on the tarmac.

As the heat rose and the cabin turned into a sweat lodge, there was precious little information. We were finally informed that the auxiliary engine had crashed. It controls all the electrical systems on the plane, including AC and ignition. Maintenance was coming to make a report. They would have the plane towed back to the gate, where they could hook up some power and give us back lights and AC. My rowmate was resourceful. She used a miniature flashlight to get to and from the restroom without incident.

Next problem. When we were pulled up to the jetway, they discovered that it wasn't working properly. So no lights and no AC. They brought up a truck to deliver AC, but all that produced was the warm heavy air that makes you feel you are under damp laundry.

By the time I had lost two pounds in sweat, they told us we would have to deplane because the auxiliary engine could not be fixed that night. As we disembarked, I heard this exchange between two airline personnel: "What are they going to do now?" "No idea." Not confidence raising.

As we milled around in the gate area, waiting to see whether we would be given another plane or be rebooked and made to stay in airline motels overnight, a fellow from my flight started talking loudly about how we would not be able to leave because of FAA "time out" regulations, which limit the number of hours airline crews can work. "Excuse me," I hailed him. "Could you put all that eloquence and imagination into talking about how magic will happen and we will get another plane tonight?"

He turned out to be a sport. After only a moment's reflection, he declared vehemently, "They are doing magic. They got us a new plane, and we will take off tonight."

He shrugged, not sure about what he had just done. Then he rushed back to the boarding gate to check. He shouted, jubilantly, "They did it! They've announced we will now depart at 9:45."

"You did it," I said. "You are a magician. You just changed the world."

There were a few more cliff-hangers. They got us boarded just before the time window closed. Now my previous rowmate and I were back in what appeared to be the same seats, the ones with impossibly spacious legroom. The new 767 seemed identical to the one we were on before. Had we simply jumped event tracks?

Our conversation quickly became rich, and often wildly funny, and deeper than the ordinary world. We talked about magical realist fiction, about how the Ottomans gave sanctuary to the Marranos when they were expelled from Spain, about soul loss and the shaman Rx for it. My rowmate turned out to be a very smart and gifted woman, doing good work all over the map to resolve conflict and promote community healing. She had explored many paths in consciousness. Her Jewish tradition had led her to study with rabbis, like David Cooper and Zalman Schachter-Shalomi, who have explored Eastern and mystical paths and sought to marry the findings of neuroscience to the understanding of how the mind interprets larger realities.

I found myself marshaling my own (limited) knowledge of Kabbala and Judaic mysticism. We were soon talking about Zalman Schachter-Shalomi's *The Dream Assembly*, stories of the Baal Shem Tov, of Abulafia and Aryeh Kaplan. She spoke with passion and knowledge about the importance of toning in Jewish mystical practice, and did not stop there. She started toning the YHVH, which is not only the Hebrew name for God, but — in some versions of Kabbalistic tradition — the secret code of the universe, the key to making or unmaking worlds.

"Hold on," I half joked. "You don't want to unmake the world by mistake."

"Oh, this is such great stuff. You do this for long enough, and it's like having sex with the Infinite."

She started toning again. It was now 1:30 AM back on the East Coast. A woman on the far side of the cabin yelled across the sleepers nested under their airline blankets. "Stop the talking over there! It's enough already."

I had never heard anyone yell across an airplane for people

to stop talking. I noted the distinctively Yiddish turn of phrase "enough already." Now whispering with my rowmate, I speculated that the protester had been mobilized by the content, more than the volume, of our conversation. "Maybe she has a point. This is high-explosive stuff. We don't want to blow up anything else tonight."

Then I was struck by an amazing life rhyme, echoing across seventeen years. At the end of 1996, I entered a series of extraordinary inner dialogues and visionary travels with a guide who started talking to me in the liminal state between waking and sleep. In my book *Dreamgates*, where I record some of these episodes, I call him, half jokingly, "G2." He seemed to speak with profound knowledge of a Western Mystery order that incorporated some elements of Kabbala. He introduced himself by telling me that we needed to begin our study sessions with the correct toning of the Tetragrammaton — an esoteric name for the four letters *YHVH* — including the hidden vowels.

How often have you heard someone tone the YHVH and talk about "sex with the Infinite" on a plane? Now I am thinking about time loops and reverse causation. Did the engine crash because of what happened later? A case of retrocausality through divine disfavor? Now *that* would be an interesting story.

WHEN I DID NOT ASK FOR ADVENTURE

"Unless something goes wrong, you don't have much of a story." I have often quoted this with appreciation.

I stopped talking this way prior to a return journey from Brazil. I had been spooked by a strange series of misadventures and long delays in flying back from Europe in mid-October, after being driven partway off a cliff by a fox-cursed demon driver on a mountain in Romania. I was trying to keep up with the progress of Hurricane Sandy, with only sketchy wifi access. So I announced to my host, when I checked my bag at Florianópolis airport, "I don't want any adventures on this trip. I'll be very happy to get home safely without a new story."

Check-in was a breeze, first at Florianópolis, then at busy São Paulo Guarulhos airport. The flights left on time, and the news was that, while New York City was a mess, Sandy had barely touched my home area 150 miles north, and my home airport was open. I relaxed in my seat for the ten-hour red-eye flight from São Paulo to Atlanta, the middle leg of my journey.

A man who spoke with an accent of the Indian subcontinent excused himself to take the window seat next to me. As soon as he had settled into his seat, he turned to me and announced, "I had an adventure."

Three days earlier, he told me, he had a major heart attack in São Paulo. He recognized the symptoms — chest pain, numbness in the left arm — because he had had a heart attack before. The hotel arranged to get him into a hospital with an excellent cardiac unit. After tests, the surgeon inserted three stents; he pulled up his right sleeve to show me where the tubes had gone in. He was able to leave the hospital the previous night, and here he was, taking a long overnight flight to Atlanta en route to his home in Arizona.

I was amazed by the speed and smoothness with which this man had apparently got through his crisis. He explained that there had been a bit of a problem. The São Paulo hospital required cash up front: one thousand reais (about five hundred dollars) to get in the door, thirty thousand dollars for the whole procedure. Fortunately for him, the company he works for had wired the money. "And if you had not been able to produce thirty thousand dollars?" "Then I would be dead."

What was he doing in Brazil? He told me he is a veterinarian who specializes in chickens. He advises on how to reduce disease risks among poultry.

I asked the chicken doctor, "What effect has this knock on the heart had on you? Will it change you in any way?"

He allowed that he might pay more attention to diet and exercise. But his response went much deeper. "I think I'll have more compassion now, because people have been kind to me. I'll spend more time with my nine-year-old daughter."

He thought a bit and added, "I'll probably find myself asking, in the face of many choices, what really matters."

I did not ask for an adventure on that trip, but I got one seated beside me.

My final flight landed early.

ANIMISTS AT THE
AIRPORT NEWSSTAND

I am walking toward a newsstand at Chicago's Midway airport to buy a bottle of water for my final flight home that evening. There are two clerks on duty, and they are talking to each other. Part of me is ready to snap at the rudeness of not paying attention to the customers.

As I near the counter, I hear the round-faced Asian clerk say this: "My grandmother told me, 'Always show respect when you go into the woods. In wartime the woods kept us safe. Take nothing from the forest, and leave nothing there, without asking permission.'" I would not mind listening to this for a long time. The name on her badge is Emilia.

The Caucasian woman at the next register looks vaguely bemused. I cannot resist. "I hope you are listening to Emilia. She's got it right."

Emilia inspects me. "Everything is alive, everything is conscious," I say. Now she looks at me as if I am family.

"You know how it is," she tells me. "When I went on the

beach and got in the water, I felt a hand from the ocean stroking my hair. It was a spirit."

"What beach?"

"In the Mariana Islands. I come from Saipan."

I tell her that in my native Australia, the Aborigines talk about the Speaking Land. We go on talking animism at the newsstand until the line gets long.

Then she stretches out both her hands. I take them, and we bless each other.

What do I say about this? I say, *Thank you.*

CHAPTER SIX

FOX TALES

Under the movement of the Fox's paws,
the earth turns.

— DOGON SAYING

Kairomancers want to dance with the Trickster. Let us spend some more time with this lord of the in-between, edgy, liminal spaces. In world folklore and myth, the Trickster takes many animal forms — as spider and coyote, as raven and squirrel — but is never confined to one form. I know him best as Fox. Fox's paw prints were all over the scene at the airport pub at the start of this book.

When Fox is around, the message is, *Pay attention.* Fox is a liminal animal, and its appearances suggest that we are entering an edgy time. Fox is at home in confusion. Fox knows when to hunt and when to hide and how to wait in concealment for the right opportunity. Fox is a master of distraction — and can succeed in distracting us when we get too sober-sided and serious about things.

Our ancestors saw Fox as a quintessential shaman spirit and ally. The oldest evidence we have of shamanism in Europe is the remains of a woman of power who was buried thirty thousand years ago inside a crypt of mammoth bones in the wooded Pavlov Hills of what is now the Czech Republic. Her body was painted red, and in her hand was placed the body of a fox, her spirit ally. The druid prince dug out of the Lindow Moss in northern England, preserved by the chemical stew of the bog, was found to be wearing an armband of red fox fur.

In China and Japan, fox spirits are both feared and propitiated. At thousands of shrines in Japan, and even in beauty salons, car dealerships, and corporate offices, you will find statues of fox guardians, often wearing red bibs, indicating that they are ready to be fed with special offerings — fried tofu is a favorite — which are constantly being supplied. The original meaning of the Japanese word for fox, *kitsune*, is "Come and sleep." It derives from the story of a fox wife (not a bad one) who revealed her true form to her husband when his dog woke her up. He loved her so much that he called her back to come and sleep.

Fox spirits can assist healers and shamans. But female fox spirits have a mixed reputation. Fox girls are believed to seduce and deceive men, though they can also bring gifts, as in the story of Lord Tadzane, who had a monk perform a dakini ritual to ensure his promotion to regent of the kingdom in 1107. A fox was sighted during these rites. Then the lord dreamed that he was visited by a woman of extraordinary beauty, with long flowing hair. He grabbed at her hair — and woke with a foxtail in his hand. He was duly made regent and created a shrine for the tail of the fox girl up on Mount Hiei.

As Trickster, Fox in Japan is said to cause people to see things that are not really there — a banquet, a battle or procession. Fox spirits are shape-shifters. They can take the form of a geisha or a monk. They are notorious for appearing as irresistibly seductive women.

In Japan, foxes are the special animals of Inari, a deity associated with divination, prosperity, and getting food on the table
— he is a patron of the rice harvest — and ordinary people say
that Inari himself is Fox, though the priests don't like to hear this.
Because of its qualities of independence and wildness, the fox in
Japan is associated with "the mystery and fundamental unruliness
of nature." Karen Smyers explains:

> Strange happenings in nature are attributed to foxes and
> badgers: rain from a sunny sky, strange lights at night, rocks
> that emit sulfuric fumes, and even volcanic eruptions. What
> unites these phenomena is not that they are necessarily bad
> or violent, but unexpected and uncontrollable. Like the
> power of nature, the original Japanese *kami* were amoral —
> potentially beneficial or destructive depending on proper
> propitiation by humans. To some degree they were syn-
> onymous with the powers of nature, or at least had these
> powers at their control. The sacred fox, similarly, cannot be
> controlled by humans.

In Anatolia and among Turkic peoples farther east, the fox is
known as a cunning, shrewd animal, and seeing one is regarded as
good luck. Kyrgyz, Yakut, and Kazakh Turks believe it is an ancestral spirit, sometimes a double or familiar. The mystics of the
Bektashi order maintain that a fox can be Khidr — the "guide of
those who have no earthly guide" — in disguise and that you are
very lucky if you see one. I learned in Turkey that the fox is also
said to be "a dervish in disguise." The animal Trickster in Turkey
is not the fox, but the coyote or jackal.

As an ally or shamanic power animal, Fox brings many gifts,
of craft and cunning, of camouflage and humor. Fox knows when
to hide and when to hunt, and how to wait in concealment for
the right opportunity. There are clues in language to the qualities

associated with Fox. To *outfox* someone is to outsmart them. *Foxy* can mean crafty, or sexy, or simply red-haired. *Shenanigan* — an act of mischief — is thought to be derived from the old Irish *sion-nachuighim*, meaning "I play the fox."

Fox is an edgy creature. In the ordinary world, we most often see foxes at dawn or at dusk, at the edge of woods and wild places. Fox is a transformer and magician among animals. This is a canine that walks like a cat, on the tips of its paws, and hunts like a cat, and has the elliptical, vertical-slit eyes of a cat. Fox is a master of camouflage and concealment. Learn from Fox how to vanish.

When Fox turns up, in dreams or in life, we want to be ready to shift. With Trickster in the field, don't try to hoe the furrows of set plans.

◆

On the night of a fire ceremony I was leading in southern France, we noticed that a Trickster energy was in play, through strange behavior and inexplicable turns of events. "Monsieur Renard est ici!" someone remarked. Every French child knows M. Renard, Mr. Fox, as the embodiment of the Trickster. None of us were surprised when a red fox started playing hide-and-seek with us, appearing and disappearing among the bushes near our gathering. Fox played this game over several hours.

At the end of that retreat, my coordinator drove me to her home near Montpellier to have dinner with her family. Her husband asked how things had gone.

"We had a wonderful time," I reported. "But Monsieur Renard was very active."

"Monsieur Renard?" Laurent exclaimed in amazement. "But he was here just five minutes ago."

He rushed to fetch a business card.

"M. RENARD," it announced in bold uppercase letters. This Mr. Fox was a landscaper who had come offering his services. We had no doubt that *the* Fox was also announcing his presence.

◆

Synchronicity can tickle like a fox's whiskers, or its brush. In California on a book tour in the spring of 2011, I felt the play of Fox magic. I sat down to lunch at a fine restaurant in Novato called the Wild Fox. At the moment I was handed the menu, adorned with the fox's face, I received an email from a friend in Europe with whom I had had no contact in nearly a year. She attached a photo of herself holding a baby fox.

In Sonoma that evening, I stopped at Ledson's Hotel, which prides itself on its selection of area wines, to see what they were pouring. When I remarked that I am a teller and lover of stories, the young sommelier asked me if I would like to hear the story of his last twenty-four hours. Certainly.

He recounted how after taking his finals the previous day, he discovered he had two flat tires. He had been feeling good about how he had done on the exams, but this did not seem like a great omen. He went around to see a friend he knew could donate a couple of old spares. The friend was out, so he waited on the porch. When the friend came home, he announced he had just won a prize in the state lottery — for hundreds, not millions, of dollars, but he was in a generous mood and proceeded to buy the soon-to-be graduate two new tires instead of giving him hand-me-downs. The day expanded into a night of conversation and interesting self-revelation that made the bartender realize, "My greatest education is coming through the book of experience."

He was proving to be a grand raconteur, but my attention was distracted by the accents of the couple seated next to me at the bar. When I asked, they told me that they were from Melbourne, Australia, my place of birth. They were in the process of touring North America in a Mustang convertible.

The sommelier had given me a lovely red wine to taste, called Mes Trois Amours. An edgy name, again suggesting that fox energy was in play. I confirmed that I'd like a full glass. When I took my first sip, he was quick to ask how I liked it. He had just realized that he had inadvertently poured a different wine from the one I had sampled. I decided to stick with the unplanned selection when I saw the label. This pinot noir was a Zina Hyde Cunningham. The last word, Cunningham, threw me back into one of my foxiest dreams, from a few years before.

In the dream, I made my way through a passage called the Cunningham Steps. The steps rose and descended at crazy angles and were sometimes missing altogether. They led over a chasm between city buildings, like a bridge. At first attempt, I could not complete the crossing. I had to reenter the dream in order to accomplish that, in a lucid-dream adventure.

When I managed to get over the Cunningham Steps, I found myself at what looked like a jolly upscale English pub, with a sign that read, "The Huntsman's Arms." When I entered, I realized at once that this was no ordinary hostelry. The publican was a red fox, dressed in a natty, tailored green jacket. The hunting prints on the wall showed a fox, in similar rig, hunting humans. The patrons of this pub were humans who had recently died. It might take them a while to wake up to their new condition.

My dream of the Fox pub at the end of the Cunningham Steps reminded me that Trickster is lord of spirit roads as well as earthly ones. He can guide traveling souls between the worlds and open passages when none seem to exist. He can take you into realms of the dead and bring the dead into realms of the living. Fox has taught me about that on other occasions.

Many years ago, I dreamed that I had a fox stuck in my throat. This coincided with a rare — and thankfully brief — period in my life when I found myself losing my voice, as if something was literally blocking my throat. Eventually, I dealt with this the old-fashioned way, the shaman's way.

With the aid of the two great black dogs (both deceased) who had shared my life and my heart and remained loyal companions on the dream roads, I tracked the fox to its earth, then pursued it down what became a long tunnel that opened into a different landscape and a different time. I was now in the British Isles, apparently in northern England. I was shown an ancient love triangle, an unwilling sacrifice, and a sacrifice refused. I saw a man die the triple druid death — in this case by a blow, by water, and by garrote — with a burned chunk of oatcake stuck in his throat. Initially an observer, I found myself able to enter the body and perspective of one of the players and felt myself shifting something, in his mind, toward the good. When I returned from that journey, I sought to apply the lessons in my current life. And I wrote up my adventures. I never had that choking problem again.

On my desk is the figure of an ancient Celt blowing a strange dragon-capped horn. Around his waist is the pelt of a red fox, head lolling at his thigh, brush hanging down his back.

◆

When I announced a playshop titled "What the Fox Knows," devoted to appreciating the Trickster element in life, I was ready for that archetype to come into play, more abundantly than ever. I was not disappointed.

Two days before I traveled to Mosswood Hollow, in an evergreen forest east of Seattle, to launch my Fox workshop, I walked a hilly path at the Esalen Institute, where I was leading another retreat. I paused to watch a black cat crossing my path. Being a contrarian, I regard a black cat on my road as a positive sign. But this was not any black cat. It had a remarkable red, bushy tail, the very semblance of a fox's brush. I was looking at a cat-fox, or a fox-cat, straight out of a mythic Trickster tale that was yet to be written. I felt, with delicious shivers, that this hybrid creature had slipped between the worlds to signal that the Fox was already in play.

I recalled how, years earlier, leading a similar retreat at Esalen, I had spoken to the group about why I regard Fox as a quintessential form of the Trickster. The group seemed to be laughing harder than my humor could explain. "Look behind you!" someone shouted. I turned, and saw only coastal cypress and the Pacific Ocean beyond the cliff. I resumed my talk, and someone yelled, "Look! He's back!" I turned again and could not see what they were talking about. They had to explain to me that whenever I spoke of Fox, a gray fox stuck its head up, looking through the window at the group while my back was turned. The fox hid itself every time I turned to see. This happened three times. There's Fox for you.

My Fox workshop at Mosswood Hollow was devoted to exploring how the Trickster can be our friend when we are willing to shift and improvise but is our devil when we insist on sticking to plans and perpetuating old habits. Part of our study was how any setback in life can prove to be an opportunity if we are prepared to look for the door that may be opening when another door slams shut or refuses to open.

A tall and beautiful redhead named Fiona joined us for the Fox workshop, bounding through the back door with sparkling confidence. Of Irish stock, now living in the Seattle area, she had decided to come only the day before, right after hearing about the workshop from a neighbor.

She did well in the journeying, to her surprise. A recurring theme for her became: interrupted life paths and parallel lives. Asked to seek the gift in a setback, she found the memory of how she resented a friend who had caused her to miss a trip to Amsterdam she thought would be wonderful twenty-five years before, when she was twenty-one. In her journey in the workshop, powered by shamanic drumming, she saw what that missed trip would have generated:

> It was as vivid as a movie. If I had taken that trip, I would have met a Canadian man. I saw the two children we would have had together. And the fire that would have destroyed our sweet country home, and the deaths of the three people I would have loved most in the world. As the only one to escape, I would have lived with survivor guilt, clinging to a rotting shack and hard memories until I died. Wow, what a gift that my friend messed up my trip all those years ago, as my life has been such a blessing!

On Saturday afternoon, she discovered she had lost the keys to her car and asked for help in searching for them. Most people joined in, searching all the places she had been on the property, reaching behind sofa cushions, scouring the floor of the yurt and the paths. Four people went through her purse after she had searched it several times. In the evening, someone used their AAA card to call a professional to open her car. The assumption was that she had locked her keys in her car, which the owner of the AAA card confessed to having done four times herself. The Triple-A man arrived after dark and popped the lock. The redhead's keys were not in the car.

She stayed at Mosswood overnight, thankful that at least she had put some things in her car on the outside chance she decided to stay overnight. She had a second car key at home but did not know where to find it since she had recently moved.

In the morning, another member of the workshop said that she had received a strong message: "Maybe you can't find the key until you know what you are supposed to unlock." This struck a chord with Fiona, who had made some breakthroughs in her thinking about relationships over the weekend, and especially in a conversation that had just happened moments ago at the breakfast table. Paul, our wonderful host at Mosswood Hollow, came to Fiona and said, "Let me check your purse again. Maybe you have a secret pocket." Fiona and Paul looked again and found the car key that wasn't there before.

Little doubt the Fox was in play, hiding something to effect certain changes. One thing Fiona noticed, during the time Fox hid her key, was that she had the active support of a whole community when she needed it, though (as she observed) it was typically outside her comfort to ask for and receive help. It warmed her heart when she looked out of the bathroom window over the frosty landscape in the early morning and saw one of our workshop participants searching her car again. "Oddly," Fiona said afterward, "I felt very calm throughout, with the feeling that everything was happening just the way it should."

The theme of parallel lives, as in Fiona's glimpse of the alternate event track that would have started in Amsterdam, became a main preoccupation for our group.

Becky asked for a dream to explore her parallel lives.

At the Sunday breakfast table, she regaled us with a marvelous story. In her dream, she is met by "Mr. Foxy," dressed like John Travolta. He tells her she must dance with him as the price of seeing what she wants to see. She is swept into a round of dirty dancing followed by tango.

Then she is offered a choice of veils of different colors. Each veil will take her into a different reality. She chooses purple and is horrified to find herself facing the teeth of a barracuda the size of a shark in an underwater world. She next chooses white and finds herself in a desert watching pilgrims advancing toward a church or mosque. She does not belong here. She chooses gold and is greeted at a carriage by a slick character she distrusts before she checks his rear and sees a fox's tail protruding from under the flaps of his tuxedo coat. She is carried into scenes of a lush life.

We had enormous fun offering feedback over breakfast. But a dream with this much life demands to be performed. So in the course of the day, we turned it into theater. Becky applauded, beaming, as the woman she had chosen to play her dream double was ground into dirty dancing by the foxiest man in the group. When it came time to check out Mr. Slick, a prankster in the circle leaped up and pushed a large stuffed toy — a fox, of course — under the back of the player's sweater so the tail hung down.

The bumper sticker was obvious, and irrepressible. In appraising a man, *Check Out His Tail.*

◆

A man named Dave in Kentucky reported in an online message that he used to think of the red fox as a harbinger of bad things because it turned up on the three worst days of his life. A skilled hunter, he set out to kill "Mr. Red," hoping to change his luck. But he could never catch the fox.

At last a friend suggested to him that the fox might actually be his "totem." When he opened to the notion that the fox could be an ally and a messenger rather than a curse, Dave found himself using fox sightings as helpful alerts. "When I see a fox now, I just smile and know my life is headed in a new direction." He added this road-tested insight: "I couldn't catch the fox because the hardest animal to find is your self."

After reading Dave's tale, I went to the family room and

turned on the TV to check the news headlines. Inexplicably, the normal settings had been changed, and I had to push buttons to get it back into TV mode. What now came on was FOX News, a channel we *never* watch — except when Fox is in play.

Befriending Fox may require the process of "gentling" that Antoine de Saint-Exupéry describes in his beloved fable *The Little Prince*, known to most of us from childhood. The fox says he can't talk to the Little Prince because he is not *apprivoisé*. In the standard English translation, this is turned into "tame." But this misses a vital level of meaning. *Apprivoiser* does not mean "to tame" in the sense of rendering an animal or person submissive or housebroken; the French language has another word for that.

The Little Prince asks three times for an explanation of this word. Eventually, the fox tells him that it means *créer des liens*, which is literally to make ties or bonds. The word could be used for a dog's leash, not something the fox is likely to want. We learn as we go along that *apprivoiser* means to befriend, to make familiar, to bring inside your home, to make gentle. This takes time, and it requires us to see from the heart, not only the eyes.

Once gentled, the fox is no longer one of a thousand foxes that hunt chickens and are pursued by hunters; he is your special friend.

"Here is my secret," the fox, gentled and befriended, says to the Little Prince. "It's quite simple: One sees clearly only with the heart. Anything essential is invisible to the eyes."

TRACKS OF THE PALE FOX

The fox of *The Little Prince* is of a genus known in West Africa as the "pale fox" or "sand fox." The Pale Fox is also a god. He is at the heart of the cosmology of the Dogon, their practice of divination, and their understanding of the play of order and chaos in the world. Let us spend a moment with this Fox.

The Dogon say that they are the conduit between heaven and earth. They remember the origins of life and human purpose in a seed star in the Sirius system that they identified long before Western astronomers were able to discover it with radio telescopes. So perhaps we should pay attention when they tell us that Fox is a god who fell to earth.

For the Dogon, the universe is a vast system of correspondences. Events in the life of an individual may enact the "amazing word of the world" — *aduno so tanie*, the lovely Dogon term for mythology — and vice versa. Their myths tell of a god named Ogo who rebelled against Amma, the All-Father of this cosmology, in the time before time, when forms were being born from the formless. After his third rebellion, when Ogo descended to what was now earth, Amma pushed him down on all fours, and he turned into the pale fox, Yurugu.

In one version of the myth, Ogo persuades Amma to spare his life by arguing that humans need divination to survive and follow the cosmic spiral. In defeat, as Fox, Ogo reveals the secrets of life, with paws rather than tongue. "Ogo remains for the Dogon even after his degradation into the Fox a revelatory being who spells out the secrets of existence." The Dogon say, "Under the movement of the Fox's paws, the earth turns."

This plays out, quite literally, in Dogon fox divination. A table with several panels is drawn in sand beyond the village fields, on the border between the settled and the wild lands, the Trickster's liminal territory. The template drawn in the sand reflects episodes in Ogo's adventures between the worlds. In each panel, the diviner traces figures representing the themes of his clients.

A team sponsored by *National Geographic* watched as a Dogon diviner drew a six-paneled tablet in the sands, at the edge of cliffs beyond the village, as the sun set. He proceeded to place tiny sticks in the panels, representing gods and spirits that might come into play. He traced designs reflecting issues and possible outcomes for the people for whom he was setting up the divination. As he drew patterns in the sand, the divination priest chanted to call Fox to make prophecy with his paws:

> Fox, speak clearly....
> Throw your traces.
> Give me your nails to mark the sand.
> Be clear. Whatever you see, tell me
> Give me your footprints.

In the morning, the diviner and the villagers returned to the site, to find that one or more foxes had walked on the tablet. The paw prints left on the sand drawing were now read to reveal the future of the community.

THE FOX AT THE EDGE OF JUNG'S GARDEN

Jung is walking in his garden at Küsnacht, on Lake Zurich, with a female patient. He likes to observe the play of natural phenomena as he talks with a client. He finds significance in every shift in the environment — a sudden wind whipping up the lake water, the shape of a cloud, the cry of a bird.

In the gentle sunlight, they walk beyond the garden, into a little wood. The woman is talking about the first dream of her life that had a huge impact on her; she calls this an "everlasting" impression. "I am in my childhood home," she recalls, "and a spectral fox is coming down the stairs." She stops and puts her hand on Jung's arm because in this moment a real fox trots out of the trees, less than forty yards in front of them. The fox proceeds to walk quietly along the path in front of them for several minutes.

Jung commented that "the animal behaves as if it were a partner in the human situation."

THE FOX AND KIM PHILBY

When the notorious spy Kim Philby was living in Beirut, working for both British intelligence and his secret controllers in the Soviet KGB, friends gave him a baby fox they had bought from Bedouin in the Jordan Valley. Philby accepted with delight, named the fox Jackie, and hand-reared her with his new wife, Eleanor. He encouraged Jackie to drink whiskey from a saucer. She slept on a sofa and came when he called her. He wrote a sentimental article about her for *Country Life* titled "The Fox Who Came to Stay."

There was an amazing convergence between the fate of the fox and Philby's downfall. In August 1962, Philby's wife came home to find him alone on the terrace of their apartment, more than usually drunk and crying his guts out. His fox had fallen — or been pushed — from the terrace and died when she hit the sidewalk five stories below. Around the same time, a woman Philby had tried to recruit for Soviet intelligence back in the 1930s decided to talk about his approach for the first time. This was the development that finally persuaded the members of the gentlemen's club in MI6 who had protected Philby for many years that they could no longer ignore the mountain of evidence that he was a traitor.

FOX'S EDGE

The notion of Fox's edge took on a sharper meaning for me on my first day up in the Carpathian mountains of Romania in the fall of 2011. With an afternoon free before I launched a workshop, my Romanian friends suggested that we should go up a nearby mountain to visit the Sphinx of Bucegi. This is a celebrated natural rock formation, held to resemble the Sphinx of Giza, that is regarded as a natural place of power with mythic associations with an ancient shaman-god of the Dacians.

The invitation was irresistible. We walked through the woods from the pleasant villa we had booked for my workshop, facing the Caraiman monastery, whose construction was inspired by a priest who dreamed of a church that needed to be built around a fir tree at this site. We intended to ride up the mountain to the sphinx by cable car, but a road cowboy with a four-wheel drive persuaded us to hire him. This proved to be the wildest ride of my life, up a steep, narrow road with hairpin bends and no railings, at the edge of dizzying cliffs. The road was often partly blocked by construction or landslides, and we often encountered cars and trucks rushing down in the middle of the road as if bent on a head-on collision.

The road cowboy drove as if possessed, but I assumed this was local custom and he knew what he was doing. I could not follow his conversation with my Romanian friends, but I was struck by his hand-waving animation as he recounted a story at a point where the road was only dirt and craters and lumps of rock. Soon after, the driver made a wild swerve to the right to get around a protruding boulder, taking us to the edge of the cliff — and then partway over. We were now stuck in the dirt, hanging over the cliff as the driver gunned the car back and forth, succeeding only in getting us deeper into the dirt, while the jeep leaned, little by little, further over the cliff.

"Time to get out of the car," I said gently.

We left the driver with the vehicle, phoning for help, and walked for twenty minutes down the winding road to a rustic inn and restaurant to recover with Ursus beer and spicy sausages. On the walk, my friends told me that just before he nearly took us all over the cliff, the driver had been boasting about how he had killed a fox on that section of mountain road and then decapitated the fox to mount its head on a wall as a trophy.

It seemed we had traveled that day with a man under a fox's curse. Through it all, I felt oddly detached, and never in real danger, as if we had been under the protection of an unseen hand.

"You know," said one of my friends. "I think that mad driver is alive because of us. The fox's curse was on him, not us. He is alive because we were there."

EACH OF OUR DAYS HAS A STORY

"Each of our days, as well as our nights, has a story," wrote Aelius Aristides, a Greek orator who walked very close to his gods.

"I own the stories," Fox declared, when he slipped into my mind during my workshop on "What the Fox Knows." Anansi makes the same claim in Neil Gaiman's brilliant comic fantasy *Anansi Boys*, inspired by West African tales of the Trickster. We do not need to concede the Trickster this much power, let alone accept his larger claims that he stole fire from heaven and made up this world.

But to dance with the Trickster and enter each day as a kairomancer requires us to be ever on the lookout for stories, the stories that make a day, the stories we are living, the stories through which we make or remake our experience of the world. We live by stories. A story is our shortest route to the meaning of things, and our easiest way to remember and carry the meaning we discover.

Making stories is a way to entertain the spirits — including our own — and to get through almost any day or disaster. If all you have are lemons, they say, make lemonade. I like to go one better. I like to make daiquiris or caipirinhas. How? By finding the story in any setback or disaster and serving it up as entertainment.

I led a workshop near the medieval town of Kernave, in Lithuania. I have seen foxes in Lithuania, but Fox was in hiding that weekend. However, his paw prints were all over the scene if you looked with inner eyes. Our hotel on the lake was charming, but there was a slight problem. Without telling my coordinator, the hotel had double-booked events. A wedding reception was being held on Saturday in the same building as my workshop. While we were drumming and dreaming upstairs, recorded music, noisy toasts, and general hoopla were rising our way from the wedding party. We were told all of this would be over by Sunday, and I drummed hard enough to push the wedding noise far from our thoughts as we made group journeys to explore ancient mysteries of the land and find pathways to personal and ancestral healing.

Surprise: on Sunday an even larger wedding party descended on the hotel. Fortunately, the sun was shining for much of the day, allowing my group to go up on the sites of the old hill forts around Kernave and dream with the eagle and the wolf and the medieval Merlin of the Baltic who came from here in a circle on the grass, with sunlight on our faces and wind in our hair. But we needed to be inside for much of the afternoon to practice the core techniques of Active Dreaming.

I returned from the afternoon break to find a wedding procession advancing toward the door of the building where we were having our workshop. There was no way to get around the wedding party. My only way to get back into our space was to join the wedding procession. I called to the dreamers watching from the terrace, "Wave!"

Then, for the first time ever, I entered a workshop space to the strains of "Here Comes the Bride."

It was not that funny at the time, but laughter came when I was able to tell it as a story. When things go wrong, remember that there may be a story brewing. Among a people of Ghana, the

Sefwi, the storyteller ends a tale like this: "Whether it be sweet or not sweet, take a bit of it, and keep the rest under your pillow." Take a bit of what you have found here, sleep on it, and in the morning, walk your dream and see what dreams the world has for you. Start your day like a kairomancer.

ACKNOWLEDGMENTS

When I journal my encounters with sidewalk oracles, I often use a running series title, "Dog Walk Chronicles." So many interesting things happen when I am out walking my dog in the street or the park or the woods, as you may have noticed in this book. I must thank my little dog, Oskar, and his late brother, Pepper, and my long-departed and beloved big black dog, Kipling, for their companionship and for two great gifts of dogs to humans: they love you no matter what, and they walk you. Kipling is the reason I regard the appearance of a friendly black dog as a very good sign, and it is because of how he appeared to me and traveled with me after his death that I am certain that dogs are soul friends on the roads of the Otherworld as well as this one.

I am grateful, yet again, to my extraordinary editor, Georgia Hughes, who keeps inviting me to write more books and makes sure that I deliver by setting the all-but-impossible deadlines that my creative daimon relishes. I tell the story here of the inspired slip that brought us together, a great example of what can happen when we remember to "Notice What's Showing through a Slip," one of my suggested everyday oracle games. It is a joy to work and play with the whole creative family at New World Library, including Tracy Cunningham, who dreams up splendid covers for my books; Kim Corbin, who helps bring them to the public with verve; and Marc Allen, who knows that dreams can come true and inspires us to manifest our best dreams.

I spend much of my life on the road, teaching and traveling all over the world map. I am grateful to all the dreamers who share in these adventures, especially those who host them. High on my list of hosts are Paul Martin and Sandie Grumman at magical Mosswood Hollow — imagine a cross between Hogwarts and Wind in the Willows — near Seattle. The kinship between my surname and the name of my favorite retreat center in North America is a striking coincidence. When Paul and Sandie created their center, out there in a hollow in the mossy redwood forest, and invented their name for it, they had never heard of me. At the time of writing, this Moss has been teaching at Mosswood Hollow for more than a decade. I am grateful to Jeni Hogenson for all the love and care with which she smoothes the ways for adventurous spirits to join me here.

I started to make a list of all the dreamers who support my work and are helping to midwife the rebirth of a dreaming society in our world, in our time. When I realized that the number of teachers of Active Dreaming alone runs to several hundred, I decided to forgo the list. I remembered the cautionary tale, from myth and folklore, of the person who tries to name all the goddesses, or all the fairies, but omits one of them, leading to all kinds of trouble with the one who was left off the list. So I shall simply say: thank you, from the heart, to all our community of active dreamers.

I give thanks for the love of family and friends.

Many thanks to *you*: dear stranger met on the road or the airplane, who shared a life story and became part of this narrative.

Praise is due to the Gatekeeper:

Lord of journeys, Lord of crossroads
Lord of many ways and many names
May our doors and gates and paths be open
And our doors and gates and paths between the worlds
And may the doors and gates and paths of any who wish
to do us or those we love any harm be closed.
May it be so.

NOTES

1. MAKING REAL MAGIC

Page 2   *a child playing with game pieces*: Charles H. Kahn, *The Art and Thought of Heraclitus: An Edition of the Fragments with Translation and Commentary* (Cambridge: Cambridge University Press, 1987), 71.

2. A WALK AROUND JUNG'S TOWER

Page 18   *The explosive force*: C. G. Jung to J. B. Rhine, 17 November 1934, in C. G. Jung, *Letters*, ed. Gerhard Adler and Aniela Jaffé, trans. R. F. C. Hull, vol. 1, *1906–1950* (Princeton, NJ: Princeton University Press, 1973), 181.

Page 18   *Someone has been pulling your leg*: C. G. Jung, *Memories, Dreams, Reflections*, ed. Aniela Jaffé, trans. Richard Winston and Clara Winston (New York: Vintage Books, 1989), 106.

Page 19   *the origin of all my ideas*: C. G. Jung, *Analytical Psychology: Notes of the Seminar Given in 1925 by C. G. Jung*, ed. William McGuire (Princeton, NJ: Princeton University Press, 1989), 6.

Page 19   *We always lose the essential*: Jorge Luis Borges, *Selected Poems*, ed. Alexander Coleman (New York: Penguin Books, 2000), 108, my free translation. Original text: *Siempre se pierde lo esencial. Es una / Ley de toda palabra sobre el numen.*

Page 20   *Cicero used the word*: Cicero, *De divinatione* 1.20.

Page 20   *non haec sine numine*: Virgil, *Aeneid* 2.777, my free translation.

Page 20   *cannot, strictly speaking*: This and the following quotes in this paragraph are from Rudolf Otto, *The Idea of the Holy: An Inquiry into the Non-rational Factor in the Idea of the Divine and Its Relation to the Rational*, trans. John W. Harvey (London: Oxford University Press, 1952), 7, 11–13.

Page 23   *took him "out of time"*: Deirdre Bair, *Jung: A Biography* (New York: Back Bay Books, 2004), 324.

Page 23   *confession in stone*: Jung, *Memories, Dreams, Reflections*, 212.

Page 24   *Jung carved the face*: Barbara Hannah, *Jung, His Life and Work: A Biographical Memoir* (Boston: Shambhala, 1991), 308.

Page 24   *That is my stone!*: Jung, *Memories, Dreams, Reflections*, 226.

Page 24   *Fairly soon, he decided*: Details in this paragraph are from Jung, *Memories, Dreams, Reflections*, 21–23.

Page 25   *Time is a child*: Ibid., 227.

Page 25   *Lifetime is a child*: Charles H. Kahn, *The Art and Thought of Heraclitus: An Edition of the Fragments with Translation and Commentary* (Cambridge: Cambridge University Press, 1987), 71.

Page 26   *He dreamed that he saw*: Hannah, *Jung*, 344.

Page 26   *Synchronicity crackled*: Details in this paragraph are from Ibid., 346, 348.

Page 26   *but clearly looking out*: Gerhard Adler, introduction to *In the Wake of Jung: A Selection of Articles from Jungian Analysts*, ed. Molly Tuby (London: Coventure, 1983), 9–10.

Page 28   *The Eastern mind*: Jean Shinoda Bolen, *The Tao of Psychology: Synchronicity and the Self* (San Francisco: Harper & Row, 1982), xi.

Page 31   *The sage...takes*: Edward L. Shaughnessy, trans. and ed., *I Ching: The Classic of Changes* (New York: Ballantine Books, 1997), 203 (italics added).

Page 32   *knows the reasons*: Ibid., 191.

Page 32   *strengthens beings and fixes*: Richard Wilhelm and Cary F. Baynes, trans., *The I Ching, or Book of Changes* (Princeton, NJ: Princeton University Press, 1990), 294.

Page 33   *The Yolngu*: Karl-Erik Sveiby and Tex Skuthorpe, *Treading Lightly: The Hidden Wisdom of the World's Oldest People* (Crows Nest, Australia: Allen & Unwin, 2006), 7.

Page 33   *the Nhunggabarra*: Ibid., 69.

Page 34   *Him good telephone*: Philip Clarke, *Where the Ancestors Walked: Australia as an Aboriginal Landscape* (Crows Nest, Australia: Allen & Unwin, 2003), 23.

Page 34   *a vibrational residue*: Robert Lawlor, *Voices of the First Day: Awakening in the Aboriginal Dreamtime* (Rochester, VT: Inner Traditions, 1991), 1.

Page 34   *Everything in the natural world*: Ibid.

Page 35   *anthropology of Spencer and Gillen*: Baldwin Spencer and F. J. Gillen, *The Arunta: A Study of a Stone Age People*, 2 vols. (London: Macmillan, 1927).

Page 35   *in Aboriginal Australia*: Sylvie Poirier, "'This Is Good Country.
We Are Good Dreamers': Dreams and Dreaming in the Australian
Western Desert," in *Dream Travelers: Sleep Experiences and Culture
in the Western Pacific*, ed. Roger Ivar Lohmann (New York: Palgrave
Macmillan, 2003), 113.

Page 35   *The spirit goes*: Ibid., 112.

Page 36   *a world full of signs*: This and the following quotes in this paragraph
are from W. E. H. Stanner, "Religion, Totemism and Symbolism," in
Aboriginal Man in Australia, ed. R. M. Berndt and C. H. Berndt (Sydney:
Angus & Robertson, 1965), 215, 227.

Page 37   *For the Nhunggabarra*: Sveiby and Skuthorpe, *Treading Lightly*, 3.

Page 39   *what we do*: This and the quotes in the following paragraph are from
Jung, *Memories, Dreams, Reflections*, 251–52.

Page 41   *Wyrd itself is constant*: Brian Bates, *The Way of Wyrd: Tales of an
Anglo-Saxon Sorcerer* (London: Century, 1983), 75.

Page 41   *Man is touched by wyrd*: Paul C. Bauschatz, *The Well and the Tree:
World and Time in Early Germanic Culture* (Amherst: University of
Massachusetts Press, 1982), 28.

Page 42   *this concept of Wyrd*: Jenny Blain, *Nine Worlds of Seid-Magic:
Ecstasy and Neo-shamanism in Northern European Paganism* (London:
Routledge, 2002), 15.

Page 42   *"reading" Wyrd, seeing*: Ibid.

Page 43   *Often I felt as though*: Ralph Metzner, *The Well of Remembrance:
Rediscovering the Earth Wisdom Myths of Northern Europe* (Boston:
Shambhala, 1994), 10.

Page 44   *rupture in time*: C. G. Jung, *C. G. Jung Speaking: Interviews and
Encounters*, ed. W. McGuire and R. F. C. Hull (London: Thames &
Hudson, 1978), 230.

3. BECOMING A KAIROMANCER

Page 50   *All things which are similar*: Heinrich Cornelius Agrippa von
Nettesheim, *Three Books of Occult Philosophy*, ed. Donald Tyson
(Woodbury, MN: Llewellyn, 1993), 413.

Page 52   *Mind and body could be*: Arthur Koestler, *The Roots of Coincidence:
An Excursion into Parapsychology* (New York: Vintage, 1973), 55.

Page 52   *ideas are projected*: Honoré de Balzac, *Louis Lambert*, trans. Clara
Bell and James Waring, Project Gutenberg, accessed April 28, 2015,
www.gutenberg.org/etext/1943.

Page 53   *We are magnets*: This and the following quotes in this paragraph are from Ralph Waldo Emerson, "Resources," in *Complete Works* (Boston: Houghton, Mifflin, 1904), vol. 8, Bartleby.com, accessed April 28, 2015, www.bartleby.com/90/0804.html.

Page 55   *creators actively court chance*: John Briggs, *Fire in the Crucible: The Alchemy of Creative Genius* (New York: St. Martin's Press, 1988), 278.

Page 55   *The writing of a book*: Roberto Calasso, *La folie Baudelaire*, trans. Alastair McEwen (New York: Farrar, Straus & Giroux, 2012), 10.

Page 56   *I found that every*: This and the quotes from AE in the following paragraph are from A. E. [George William Russell], *The Candle of Vision: Inner Worlds of the Imagination* (1918; Bridport, England: Prism Press, 1990), 9–10.

Page 56   *I feel I belong*: P. L. Travers, "The Death of AE," in *What the Bee Knows: Reflections on Myth, Symbol and Story* (London: Arkana, 1994), 244–45.

Page 62   *the imagination is*: Letter to Alphonse Toussenel, 1858, in Calasso, *La folie Baudelaire*, 11–12.

Page 65   *In the beginning*: Ben Okri, *The Famished Road* (New York: Anchor Books, 1993), 3.

Page 69   *Harriet Tubman*: Robert Moss, *The Secret History of Dreaming* (Novato, CA: New World Library, 2009), 182–88.

Page 69   *the compensations of calamity*: This and the following quote in this paragraph are from Ralph Waldo Emerson, "Compensation," in *The Essential Writings of Ralph Waldo Emerson*, ed. Brooks Atkinson (New York: Modern Library, 2000), 170–71.

Page 70   *If there is divination*: Cicero, *Cicero on Divination: De divinatione, Book 1*, trans. David Wardle (Oxford: Clarendon Press, 2006), 108.

Page 70   *exerted a hold on Freud*: Janine Burke, *The Gods of Freud: Sigmund Freud's Art Collection* (Milsons Point, Australia: Knopf, 2006).

Page 70   *The Spirit of Psychology*: English translation of Jung's "Der Geist der Psychologie," in Joseph Campbell, ed., *Spirit and Nature: Eranos Yearbook 1954* (Princeton, NJ: Princeton University Press, 1954).

Page 72   *swooping down from the sky*: This and the following quotes from the *Odyssey* in this chapter are taken from Homer, *The Odyssey*, trans. Robert Fagles (New York: Penguin Books, 1997).

Page 75   *The poet marries*: Quoted in Rollo May, *The Courage to Create* (New York: Norton, 1994), 85.

Page 79   *It is not hard to keep*: Neil Gaiman, *Anansi Boys: A Novel* (New York: HarperTorch, 2005), 181.

Page 79   *Alan Vaughan tells*: Alan Vaughan's story is from his *Incredible*

Coincidence: The Baffling World of Synchronicity (New York: New American Library, 1979), 121–22.

Page 80   *Mitchell relates*: Sam Jordison, "David Mitchell's Unusual Adventure into History," *Guardian*, June 24, 2014.

Page 81   *Caminante, no hay camino*: Antonio Machado, "Proverbios y cantares XXIX" [Proverbs and Songs 29], in *Campos de Castilla* [The Landscape of Castile] (1917; reprint, Buffalo, NY: White Pine Press, 2005), 238.

4. THE BOOK OF SIDEWALK ORACLES

Page 84   *Karen Smyers visited*: Karen A. Smyers, *The Fox and the Jewel: Shared and Private Meanings in Contemporary Japanese Inari Worship* (Honolulu: University of Hawaii Press, 1999), 4–5.

Page 93   *anthropologist Mubuy Mpier*: Mubuy Mubay Mpier, "Dreams among the Yansi," in *Dreaming, Religion and Society in Africa*, ed. M. C. Jedrej and Rosalind Shaw (New York: Brill, 1992), 100–111.

Page 93   *We do not always*: Mary Watkins, *Waking Dreams* (Dallas, TX: Spring, 1992), 141.

Page 93   *You not only see*: Kathleen Raine, *Defending Ancient Springs* (London: Oxford University Press, 1967), 113.

Page 101   *a recurrence of the same*: Arthur Koestler, *The Roots of Coincidence: An Excursion into Parapsychology* (New York: Vintage, 1973), 95.

Page 101   *a quasi-gravitational attraction*: Ibid., 110.

Page 104   *At Pharai in the Peloponnese*: Robert Moss, *Conscious Dreaming: A Spiritual Path for Everyday Life* (New York: Three Rivers Press, 1996), 166–68.

Page 104   *the friendliest of gods*: Ibid., 167.

Page 107   *Crows communicate*: John M. Marzluff and Tony Angell, *In the Company of Crows and Ravens* (New Haven, CT: Yale University Press, 2005), 196.

Page 109   *king named Tarquinius*: For the story of Tarquinius and the sibyl, see Dianne Skafte, *When Oracles Speak: Opening Yourself to Messages Found in Dreams, Signs, and the Voices of Nature* (London: Thorsons, 1997), 173–74.

Page 112   *If we love*: Robert Browning and Elizabeth Barrett Browning, *The Letters of Robert Browning and Elizabeth Barrett Barrett, 1845–1846*, ed. Elvan Kinter, vol. 1, *January 1845 to March 1846* (Cambridge, MA: Harvard University Press, 2004), 470.

Page 113   *My dear Mrs. Crowley*: C. G. Jung to Alice Lewisohn Crowley, 20

July 1942, in C. G. Jung, *Letters*, ed. Gerhard Adler and Aniela Jaffé, trans. R. F. C. Hull, vol. 1, *1906–1950* (Princeton, NJ: Princeton University Press, 1973), 319.

Page 118 *There is no energy*: C. G. Jung, *Two Essays on Analytical Psychology*, trans. R. F. C. Hull (Princeton, NJ: Princeton University Press, 1972), 53–54.

Page 120 *I had sweet company*: A. E. [George William Russell], *Collected Poems*, 2nd ed. (London: Macmillan, 1926), 230.

Page 122 *The* Book of the Road: W. F. Ryan, *The Bathhouse at Midnight: An Historical Survey of Magic and Divination in Russia* (University Park, PA: Penn State University Press, 2011), 123–24.

Page 122 *We talked, and although*: Jung in conversation with Miguel Serrano, September 1960, C. G. Jung, *C. G. Jung Speaking: Interviews and Encounters*, ed. W. McGuire and R. F. C. Hull (London: Thames & Hudson, 1978), 464–65.

Page 126 *When two people meet*: Jean Shinoda Bolen, *The Tao of Psychology: Synchronicity and the Self* (San Francisco: Harper & Row, 1982), 51.

Page 128 *Think not you can direct:* Khalil Gibran, "Love," in *The Prophet*, Wikilivres, last modified August 10, 2010, http://wikilivres.ca/wiki /The_Prophet/Love.

Page 133 *Exoriare aliquis nostris*: Virgil, *Aeneid* 4.625.

Page 135 *If I had his nuts*: Mark Twain, *Autobiography of Mark Twain*, ed. Harriet Elinor Smith et al. (Berkeley: University of California Press, 2010), 1:106 (italics in the original).

Page 136 *could persuade a fish*: Ron Powers, *Mark Twain: A Life* (New York: Free Press, 2005), 545.

Page 144 *In surveys, 75–92 percent*: Arthur Funkhouser and Michael Schredl, "The Frequency of Déjà Vu (Déjà Rêve) and the Effects of Age, Dream Recall Frequency and Personality Factors," *International Journal of Dream Research* 3, no. 1 (2010): 60.

Page 144 *survey of 444 students*: Ibid.

Page 146 *Émile Boirac*: Émile Boirac, *The Psychology of the Future*, trans. and ed. W. de Kerlor (London: Kegan Paul, 1918), 233.

Page 146 *Almost any mental tempest*: Frederic W. H. Myers, "The Subliminal Self, Chapter 8: The Relation of Supernormal Phenomena to Time; Retrocognition," *Proceedings of the Society for Psychical Research* 11 (1895): 354.

Page 146 *a suddenly evoked reminiscence*: Ibid., 341.

Page 148 *as if someone were at my ear*: Paul Edwards, *Reincarnation: A Critical Examination* (Amherst, NY: Prometheus Books, 2001), 54.

Page 148 *At sunset, when I*: Charles Dickens, *Pictures from Italy* (London: Penguin Classics, 1998), 73–74.

Page 153 *This being human*: Coleman Barks et al., trans., *The Essential Rumi* (San Francisco: HarperSanFrancisco, 1995), 109.

Page 153 *treat each guest honorably*: Ibid.

Page 161 *In Cicero's time*: Cicero, *Cicero on Divination: De divinatione, Book 1*, trans. David Wardle (Oxford: Clarendon Press, 2006), 118.

Page 166 *Victor Hugo did not like*: Graham Robb, *Victor Hugo: A Biography* (New York: Norton, 2007), 459.

Page 166 *When Hugo moved back*: Ibid., 494.

Page 185 *Mark Twain developed*: Robert Moss, *The Secret History of Dreaming* (Novato, CA: New World Library, 2009), 200–202.

6. FOX TALES

Page 211 *The oldest evidence*: Barbara Tedlock, *The Woman in the Shaman's Body: Reclaiming the Feminine in Religion and Medicine* (New York: Bantam Books, 2005), 3–4.

Page 212 *The druid prince*: Anne Ross and Don Robbins, *The Life and Death of a Druid Prince* (New York: Summit Books, 1989), 57–59.

Page 212 *the Japanese word for fox*: Karen A. Smyers, *The Fox and the Jewel: Shared and Private Meanings in Contemporary Japanese Inari Worship* (Honolulu: University of Hawaii Press, 1999), 72.

Page 212 *the story of Lord Tadzane*: Ibid., 84.

Page 213 *the mystery and fundamental*: Ibid., 98.

Page 213 *Strange happenings in nature*: Ibid.

Page 222 *Here is my secret*: Antoine de Saint-Exupéry, *The Little Prince*, trans. Richard Howard (New York: Mariner Books, 2000), 63.

Page 223 *Ogo remains for the Dogon*: Roger D. Pelton, *The Trickster in West Africa: A Study of Mythic Irony and Sacred Delight* (Berkeley: University of California Press, 1980), 207.

Page 223 *Under the movement*: Marcel Griaule and Germaine Dieterlen, *Le renard pâle*, vol. 1, *Le mythe cosmogonique* (Paris: Institut d'Ethnologie, 1948), 280, my free translation.

Page 223 *A team sponsored*: The *National Geographic* account of the Dogon diviner is from Chris Rainier, "Unique Dogon Culture Survives in West Africa," *National Geographic News*, May 29, 2003, http://news.nationalgeographic.com/news/2003/05/0529_030529_dogon.html.

Page 224 *an "everlasting" impression*: The quotes in this and the following paragraph are from C. G. Jung, *Letters*, ed. Gerhard Adler and Aniela

Jaffé, trans. R. F. C. Hull, vol. 1, *1906–1950* (Princeton, NJ: Princeton University Press, 1973), 395.

Page 225   *In August 1962*: Ben Macintyre, *A Spy among Friends: Kim Philby and the Great Betrayal* (New York: Crown, 2014), 230–31, 241.

Page 227   *Each of our days*: P. Aelius Aristides, *The Complete Works*, trans. Charles A. Behr, vol. 2, *Orations XVII–LIII* (Leiden: Brill, 1981), 279.

Page 229   *Whether it be sweet*: Alexander Eliot, *The Timeless Myths: How Ancient Legends Influence the Modern World* (New York: Truman Talley Books, 1996), 23.

SELECT BIBLIOGRAPHY

Aziz, Robert. *C. G. Jung's Psychology of Religion and Synchronicity*. Albany: State University of New York Press, 1990.

Bates, Brian. *The Way of Wyrd: Tales of an Anglo-Saxon Sorcerer*. London: Century, 1983.

———. *The Wisdom of Wyrd: Teachings for Today from Our Ancient Past*. London: Rider, 1996.

Baudelaire, Charles. *The Complete Verse*. Translated by Francis Scarfe. London: Anvil Press Poetry, 1986.

———. *The Painter of Modern Life and Other Essays*. Translated and edited by Jonathan Mayne. London: Phaidon Press, 1995.

Bauschatz, Paul C. *The Well and the Tree: World and Time in Early Germanic Culture*. Amherst: University of Massachusetts Press, 1982.

Beard, Mary. "Cicero and Divination: The Formation of a Latin Discourse." *Journal of Roman Studies* 76 (1986): 33–46.

Berndt, R. M., and C. H. Berndt. *Man, Land and Myth in North Australia: The Gunwinggu People*. Sydney: Ure Smith, 1970.

———. *The Speaking Land: Myth and Story in Aboriginal Australia*. Rochester, VT: Inner Traditions, 1994.

Blain, Jenny. *Nine Worlds of Seid-Magic: Ecstasy and Neo-shamanism in Northern European Paganism*. London: Routledge, 2002.

Blair, Deirdre. *Jung: A Biography*. New York: Back Bay Books, 2003.

Bolen, Jean Shinoda. *The Tao of Psychology: Synchronicity and the Self*. San Francisco: Harper & Row, 1982.

Borges, Jorge Luis. *Collected Fictions*. Translated by Andrew Hurley. New York: Penguin Books, 1998.

————. *Selected Non-fictions*. Edited by Eliot Weinberger. Translated by
    Ester Allen, Suzanne Jill Levine, and Eliot Weinberger. New York:
    Penguin Books, 1999.

————. *Twenty-Four Conversations with Borges, Including a Selection of
    Poems: Interviews by Roberto Alifano 1981–1983*. Translated by Nicomedes
    Suárez Araúz, Willis Barnstone, and Noemí Escandell. Housatonic, MA:
    Lascaux, 1984.

Boyd, Brian. *On the Origin of Stories: Evolution, Cognition, and Fiction*.
    Cambridge, MA: Harvard University Press, 2009.

Braud, William. "The Farther Reaches of Psi Research: Future Choices and
    Possibilities." In *Parapsychology in the Twenty-First Century: Essays on the
    Future of Psychical Research*, edited by Michael A. Thalbourne and Lance
    Storm, 38–64. Jefferson, NC: McFarland, 2005.

Brotchie, Alastair, and Mel Gooding, eds. *A Book of Surrealist Games*. Boston:
    Shambhala, 1995.

Burke, Janine. *The Gods of Freud: Sigmund Freud's Art Collection*. Milsons
    Point, Australia: Knopf, 2006.

Calasso, Roberto. *Ka: Stories of the Mind and Gods of India*. New York: Knopf,
    1998.

————. *La Folie Baudelaire*. Translated by Alastair McEwen. New York:
    Farrar, Straus & Giroux, 2012.

————. *The Marriage of Cadmus and Harmony*. Translated by Tim Parks.
    New York: Vintage, 1994.

Calderón de la Barca, Pedro. *La vida es sueño*. Madrid: Espasa-Calpe, 1969.

Cambray, Joseph. *Synchronicity: Nature and Psyche in an Interconnected
    Universe*. College Station: Texas A&M University Press, 2009.

Campbell, Joseph. *The Hero with a Thousand Faces*. 3rd ed. Novato, CA:
    New World Library, 2008.

————. *Myths to Live By*. New York: Bantam Books, 1988.

Cicero. *Cicero on Divination: De divinatione, Book 1*. Translated by David
    Wardle. Oxford: Clarendon Press, 2006.

————. *The Nature of the Gods*. Translated by Horace C. P. McGregor.
    London: Penguin Books, 1988.

Clarke, Philip. *Where the Ancestors Walked: Australia as an Aboriginal
    Landscape*. Crows Nest, Australia: Allen & Unwin, 2003.

Combs, Allan, and Mark Holland. *Synchronicity: Science, Myth, and the
    Trickster*. New York: Paragon House, 1990.

Csikszentmihalyi, Mihaly. *Flow: The Psychology of Optimal Experience*. New
    York: Harper & Row, 1990.

Dossey, Larry. *The Science of Premonitions: How Knowing the Future Can Help*

Us Avoid Danger, Maximize Opportunities, and Create a Better Life. New York: Plume, 2009.

Eliade, Mircea. *Journal I, 1945–1955*. Translated by Mac Linscott Ricketts. Chicago: University of Chicago Press, 1984.

———. *Myth and Reality*. Translated by Willard R. Trask. New York: Harper & Row, 1975.

———. *Myths, Dreams, and Mysteries: The Encounter between Contemporary Faiths and Archaic Realities*. Translated by Philip Mairet. New York: Harper & Row, 1975.

———. *The Sacred and the Profane: The Nature of Religion*. Translated by Willard R. Trask. New York: Harcourt, Brace, 1987.

Eliot, Alexander. *The Timeless Myths: How Ancient Legends Influence the Modern World*. New York: Truman Talley Books, 1996.

Emerson, Ralph Waldo. *The Essential Writings of Ralph Waldo Emerson*. Edited by Brooks Atkinson. New York: Modern Library, 2000.

Evans-Wentz, W. Y. *The Fairy Faith in Celtic Countries*. New York: Citadel Press, 1990.

Franck, Frederick. *The Zen of Seeing: Drawing as Meditation*. New York: Vintage Books, 1973.

Freud, Sigmund. *The Psychopathology of Everyday Life*. Translated by A. A. Brill. London: E. Benn, 1935.

Gaiman, Neil. *American Gods: A Novel*. New York: HarperTorch, 2002.

———. *Anansi Boys: A Novel*. New York: HarperTorch, 2005.

Geary, James. *I Is an Other: The Secret Life of Metaphor and How It Shapes the Way We See the World*. New York: Harper Perennial, 2011.

Gieser, Suzanne. *The Innermost Kernel: Depth Psychology and Quantum Physics; Wolfgang Pauli's Dialogue with C. G. Jung*. Heidelberg: Springer-Verlag, 2005.

Griaule, Marcel, and Germaine Dieterlen. *Le renard pâle*. Vol. 1, *Le mythe cosmogonique*. Paris: Institut d'Ethnologie, 1948.

Hannah, Barbara. *Jung, His Life and Work: A Biographical Memoir*. Boston: Shambhala, 1991.

Haupt, Lyanda Lynn. *Crow Planet: Essential Wisdom from the Urban Wilderness*. New York: Little, Brown, 2009.

Herodotus. *The Histories*. Translated by Aubrey de Sélincourt. Harmondsworth, England: Penguin, 1982.

Hollander, Lee M., trans. *The Poetic Edda*. Austin: University of Texas Press, 1987.

Homer. *The Odyssey*. Translated by Robert Fagles. New York: Penguin Books, 1997.

Houston, Jean. *The Hero and the Goddess: The Odyssey as Mystery and Initiation*. New York: Ballantine Books, 1992.

Hyde, Lewis. *Trickster Makes This World: Mischief, Myth, and Art*. New York: Farrar, Straus & Giroux, 1998.

Jaffé, Aniela. *Apparitions and Precognition: A Study from the Point of View of C. G. Jung's Analytical Psychology*. New Hyde Park, NY: University Books, 1963.

James, Tony. *Dream, Creativity, and Madness in Nineteenth-Century France*. Oxford: Oxford University Press, 1995.

Johnson, Kij. *The Fox Woman*. New York: Tor, 2000.

Jung, C. G. *The Archetypes and the Collective Unconscious*. Translated by R. F. C. Hull. Princeton, NJ: Princeton University Press, 1980.

———. *C. G. Jung Speaking: Interviews and Encounters*. Edited by W. McGuire and R. F. C. Hull. London: Thames & Hudson, 1978.

———. *Children's Dreams: Notes from the Seminar Given in 1936–1940*. Translated by Ernst Falzeder. Princeton, NJ: Princeton University Press, 2008.

———. *Letters*. Edited by Gerhard Adler and Aniela Jaffé. Translated by R. F. C. Hull. Vol. 1, *1906–1950*. Princeton, NJ: Princeton University Press, 1973.

———. *Memories, Dreams, Reflections*. Edited by Aniela Jaffé. Translated by Richard Winston and Clara Winston. New York : Vintage Books, 1989.

———. *The Red Book: Liber Novus*. Edited by Sonu Shamdasani. New York: Norton, 2009.

———. *Synchronicity: An Acausal Connecting Principle*. Translated by R. F. C. Hull. Princeton, NJ: Princeton University Press, 1973.

———. *Two Essays on Analytical Psychology*. Translated by R. F. C. Hull. Princeton, NJ: Princeton University Press, 1972.

Kahn, Charles H. *The Art and Thought of Heraclitus: An Edition of the Fragments with Translation and Commentary*. Cambridge: Cambridge University Press, 1987.

Koestler, Arthur. *The Roots of Coincidence: An Excursion into Parapsychology*. New York: Vintage, 1973.

Landon, Carolyn, and Eileen Harrison. *Black Swan: A Koorie Woman's Life*. Crows Nest, Australia: Allen & Unwin, 2011.

Long, Max Freedom. *The Secret Science behind Miracles*. Marina del Rey, CA: DeVorss, 1976.

Mabille, Pierre. *Mirror of the Marvelous: The Classic Surrealist Work on Myth*. Translated by Jody Gladding. Rochester, VT: Inner Traditions, 1998.

Mansfield, Victor. *Synchronicity, Science, and Soul-Making: Understanding*

Jungian Synchronicity through Physics, Buddhism, and Philosophy. Chicago: Open Court, 1998.

Meier, C. A., ed. *Atom and Archetype: The Pauli/Jung Letters, 1932–1958*. Translated by David Roscoe. Princeton, NJ: Princeton University Press, 2001.

Metzner, Ralph. *The Well of Remembrance: Rediscovering the Earth Wisdom Myths of Northern Europe*. Boston: Shambhala, 1994.

Moore, Virginia. *The Unicorn: William Butler Yeats' Search for Reality*. New York: Macmillan, 1954.

Moss, Robert. *Active Dreaming: Journeying Beyond Self-Limitation to a Life of Wild Freedom*. Novato, CA: New World Library, 2012.

———. *Conscious Dreaming: A Spiritual Path for Everyday Life*. New York: Three Rivers Press, 1996.

———. *The Dreamer's Book of the Dead: A Soul Traveler's Guide to Death, Dying, and the Other Side*. Rochester, VT: Destiny Books, 2005.

———. *Dreamgates: Exploring the Worlds of Soul, Imagination, and Life Beyond Death*. Novato, CA: New World Library, 2010.

———. *Dreaming True: How to Dream Your Future and Change Your Life for the Better*. New York: Pocket Books, 2000.

———. *Dreamways of the Iroquois: Honoring the Secret Wishes of the Soul*. Rochester, VT: Destiny Books, 2005.

———. *Here, Everything Is Dreaming: Poems and Stories*. Albany, NY: Excelsior, 2013.

———. *The Secret History of Dreaming*. Novato, CA: New World Library, 2009.

———. *The Three "Only" Things: Tapping the Power of Dreams, Coincidence & Imagination*. Novato, CA: New World Library, 2007.

Needham, Joseph. *Science and Civilisation in China*. Vol. 2, *History of Scientific Thought*. Cambridge: Cambridge University Press, 1956.

Otto, Rudolf. *The Idea of the Holy: An Inquiry into the Non-rational Factor in the Idea of the Divine and Its Relation to the Rational*. Translated by John W. Harvey. London: Oxford University Press, 1952.

Peat, F. David. *Synchronicity: The Bridge between Matter and Mind*. New York: Bantam Books, 1988.

Pelton, Roger D. *The Trickster in West Africa: A Study of Mythic Irony and Sacred Delight*. Berkeley: University of California Press, 1980.

Pike, Diane Kennedy. *Life as a Waking Dream*. New York: Riverhead Books, 1997.

Poirier, Sylvie. "'This Is Good Country. We Are Good Dreamers': Dreams and Dreaming in the Australian Western Desert." In *Dream Travelers:*

Sleep Experiences and Culture in the Western Pacific, edited by Roger Ivar Lohmann, 107–26. New York: Palgrave Macmillan, 2003.

Powers, Ron. *Mark Twain: A Life*. New York: Free Press, 2005.

Radin, Dean. *Entangled Minds: Extrasensory Experiences in a Quantum Reality*. New York: Paraview Pocket Books, 2006.

Reid, Bill, and Robert Bringhurst. *The Raven Steals the Light*. Toronto: Douglas & McIntyre, 1996.

Robb, Graham. *Victor Hugo: A Biography*. New York: Norton, 2007.

Roberts, Jane. *The Education of Oversoul 7*. New York: Pocket Books, 1976.

———. *The Nature of Personal Reality: Specific, Practical Techniques for Solving Everyday Problems and Enriching the Life You Know*. New York: Bantam Books, 1990.

———. *Seth Speaks: The Eternal Validity of the Soul*. Novato, CA: New World Library, 1994.

Ryan, W. F. *The Bathhouse at Midnight: An Historical Survey of Magic and Divination in Russia*. University Park, PA: Penn State University Press, 2011.

Schofield, Malcolm. "Cicero for and against Divination." *Journal of Roman Studies* 76 (1986): 47–65.

Schopenhauer, Arthur. *Parerga and Paralipomena: Short Philosophical Essays*. Translated by E. F. J. Payne. Oxford: Oxford University Press, 1974.

Shaughnessy, Edward L., trans. and ed. *I Ching: The Classic of Changes*. New York: Ballantine Books, 1997.

Smyers, Karen A. *The Fox and the Jewel: Shared and Private Meanings in Contemporary Japanese Inari Worship*. Honolulu: University of Hawaii Press, 1999.

Sommer, Bettina Sejbjerg. "The Norse Concept of Luck." *Scandinavian Studies* 79, no. 3 (2007): 275–94.

Stanner, W. E. H. *The Dreaming & Other Essays*. Collingwood, Australia: Black Ink, 2011.

Sveiby, Karl-Erik, and Tex Skuthorpe. *Treading Lightly: The Hidden Wisdom of the World's Oldest People*. Crows Nest, Australia: Allen & Unwin, 2006.

Talbot, Michael. *The Holographic Universe: The Revolutionary Theory of Reality*. New York: Harper Perennial, 1992.

Tarnas, Richard. *Cosmos and Psyche: Intimations of a New World View*. New York: Plume, 2007.

Temple, Robert. *Oracles of the Dead: Ancient Techniques for Predicting the Future*. Rochester, VT: Destiny Books, 2005.

Titchenell, Elsa-Britta. *The Masks of Odin: Wisdom of the Ancient Norse*. Pasadena, CA: Theosophical University Press, 2008.

Tuby, Molly, ed. *In the Wake of Jung: A Selection of Articles from Jungian Analysts*. London: Coventure, 1983.

Vaughan, Alan. *Incredible Coincidence: The Baffling World of Synchronicity*. New York: New American Library, 1979.

von Franz, Marie-Louise. *On Divination and Synchronicity: The Psychology of Meaningful Chance*. Toronto: Inner City Books, 1990.

Wilhelm, Richard, and Cary F. Baynes, trans. *The I Ching, or Book of Changes*. Princeton, NJ: Princeton University Press, 1990.

Winterbourne, Anthony. *When the Norns Have Spoken: Time and Fate in Germanic Paganism*. Madison, NJ: Fairleigh Dickinson University Press, 2004.

Yeats, W. B. *Autobiography*. New York: Collier Books, 1965.

———. *Collected Poems*. London: Macmillan, 1958.

———. *Mythologies*. New York: Macmillan, 1959.

INDEX

Abbott, Edwin Abbott, 194
Acedia (noonday demon), 155
Active Dreaming circles, 174–75
Adams, Douglas, 171–72
Adirondack Mountains, 174
AE. *See* Russell, George ("AE")
Aeneid (Virgil), 20
Agrippa von Nettesheim, Heinrich
    Cornelius, 50
air travel: chance encounters during,
    124–25; Kairos moments during,
    187–209
Akwesasne (Mohawk reservation), 164
Alaric (Goth leader), 110
Albertus Magnus, 51–52
Albright, Madeleine, 187
Alcheringa (Dream Times), 35
Alice's Adventures in Wonderland (Carroll),
    3
alternate event tracks. *See* parallel event
    tracks
ambiguity, tolerance for, 61
American Civil War, 60, 69
Amma (Dogon deity), 223
Anansi (West African deity), 79, 227
Anansi Boys (Gaiman), 79, 227
Anatolia (Turkey), 177, 182, 213
Ancestors, 34–36
Angell, Tony, 107
angelology, 112
angels, 123–24
anger, 155

animal sacrifice, 86
animism, 208–9
anticipatory symptoms, 168–73
Anubis (Egyptian deity), 78, 157
anxiety, 155
archery, *kairos* in, 48
archetypes, 70–71, 77–80
Aristotle, 61
Artemidorus, 61
Ashanti people, 79
Asklepios (Greek patron of dream healing),
    24
Association of the Study of Dreams confer-
    ence (New York, NY; 2000), 174
Athena (Greek deity), 71–73
Athenians, 200
attitude, choice of, 50–53, 203
attraction, law of, 13, 50
Auden, W. H., 75–76
Austin (TX) poster campaign, 42
Australian Aborigines: Ancestors of, 34–36;
    Dreaming/Dreamtime of, 34–37;
    Speaking Land of, 33–34, 36, 37,
    59–60, 209
Australian National University, 200
Autobiography (Twain), 135–36
Autobiography (Yeats), 119

Bali, 66–67
Balzac, Honoré de, 52–53
"Banana Boat Song, The" (song), 140–41
Barks, Coleman, 114

ABOUT THE AUTHOR

Robert Moss is the creator of Active Dreaming, an original synthesis of modern dreamwork and shamanism. Born in Australia, he survived three near-death experiences in childhood. He leads popular workshops all over the world, including a three-year training for teachers of Active Dreaming and online courses for the Shift Network. A former lecturer in ancient history at the Australian National University, he is a *New York Times* bestselling novelist, poet, journalist, and independent scholar. His many books on dreaming, shamanism, and imagination include *Conscious Dreaming*, *The Secret History of Dreaming*, *Dreaming the Soul Back Home*, and *The Boy Who Died and Came Back*. He has lived in upstate New York since he received a message from a red-tailed hawk under an old white oak.

His website is www.mossdreams.com.